CREATIVE
FAMILY
ACTIVITIES

CREATIVE FAMILY ACTIVITIES

Valerie Sloane

ABINGDON
Nashville

CREATIVE FAMILY ACTIVITIES

Copyright © 1976 by Abingdon

All rights reserved

Library of Congress Cataloging in Publication Data
Sloane, Valerie, 1935-
    Creative family activities.
    1. Parent and child. 2. Family recreation. 3.
Creative activities and seat work. I. Title.
HQ755.85.S55   649'.51   75-45208

ISBN 0-687-09828-9

Part of "Mystery Car-Rides" appeared as "Destination Unknown" in *Chevron USA*, Summer 1971.

Part of "Organizational Guide for Traveling Parents" appeared as "When Mother Travels" in *Mothers' Manual*, September/October 1972, and is reprinted with permission of *Mothers' Manual* magazine © 1972.

Part of the section on filling out forms, originally entitled "What Your Child Doesn't Know Might Hurt Him," is reprinted by permission of *Junior Bowler*.

MANUFACTURED BY THE PARTHENON PRESS AT
NASHVILLE, TENNESSEE, UNITED STATES OF AMERICA

Dedicated to Howard, Perri, Hal, and the two Grandmas, Ruth and Amy, all of whom made this book possible.

Preface

Most men and women have no prior training for the formidable responsibility of being parents. They are called upon to be experts in child development, specialists in human psychology, and masters at skills they have never been taught.

Their task can be a rewarding challenge, however, when tackled with open minds and fresh ideas.

Parents must look at their offspring through imaginative eyes and ask, "How can we creatively motivate this child who says, 'I hate to read'? How can we cleverly quiet these bouncing young travelers in the back of our family car? How can we skillfully accommodate the three children who are eager to cook in our kitchen?"

Though some parents would deny it, noted authorities agree that creativity is present in every human being, even though it may be suppressed.

Family life offers endless opportunities for that creativity to surface.

Children spend approximately 6,570 days in residence in the family home. There are Fundays and Sundays, Shirkdays and Workdays, Feeding Times and Needing Times.

PREFACE

The activities suggested in this book offer new ways to make those days pleasant and productive for both parents and children. They are intended to stimulate the reader's creativity and to inspire untried methods. Hopefully they will keep children from writing on the walls and parents from climbing them.

On to creative family activities!

Contents

PART THREE

Shirk Days

PART FOUR

Workdays

PART FIVE

Feeding Times

PART SIX

Needing Times

Oh, how we need ideas for leading children through the wilderness of infancy, through the jungles of adolescence, to the land of maturity!

—Alex F. Osborn, *Applied Imagination*

PART ONE

FUNDAYS

Many of us think of creativity in terms of great works of art, music, literature or science. But we frequently overlook that creativity blossoming in small ways is just as authentic as creativity expressed in a grand manner.

> —Dorothy Corkille Briggs, *Your Child's Self-Esteem*

The Backyard Carnival

"There's nothing to do!" is one of the most frequent cries of childhood. Yet any helpful suggestions by parents referring to a closet full of toys or a shelf full of games will probably be flatly rejected.

The most desirable activities for young people are those in which they become totally involved over an extended period of time. This need for involvement can be fulfilled by building a model, putting together a puzzle, or making a blouse.

One family recalls a project the children became involved in while the parents painted the house. To keep his younger brother and sister out of the paint and out of the way, the sixteen-year-old boy offered to organize a backyard carnival for the neighborhood children. On one of those rare occasions when three children in a family agree, the two younger ones reacted enthusiastically to their brother's idea. During that week the parents took a break from their brushes and stepped outside to witness this scene in their bannered backyard:

Their eleven-year-old daughter, resplendent in purple rouge, green beads, and a red cloth wrapped around her head, was staring at the palm-upturned hand of the neighbors' boy. She told him he had a long lifeline then gazed into a marmalade jar turned crystal ball. "Your father won't be crabby today. You'll be in first grade soon," the fortune-teller said. The satisfied customer proceeded to the next attraction at the carnival.

In planning the carnival attractions the teen-ager and his brother and sister followed five major steps.

Gathering Prizes

Prizes were found by cleaning out drawers and closets rather than by spending money. An excess accumulation of squishy rubber monsters, miniature cars, and unused coloring books was gaily wrapped in blue cellophane and assembled in one of the booths. Prizes were categorized according to the number of win tickets required for each item. When they ran out of prizes the children called the carnival to a startling halt and rummaged through their drawers for more treasures.

Advertising and Tickets

The children spread word of the approaching carnival throughout the neighborhood. A flyer patterned after the following was distributed:

```
CARNIVAL

At 210 Oak Avenue .....................
Thursday and Friday, July 19 and 20 ........
2 until 6 P.M. ........7 until 9 P.M. ...........
Bring money for tickets and refreshments ....
Win prizes ........Play games ..............
Fantastic door prizes .....................
Have your fortune told ....................
Bring friends ..............................

          Larry, Karen, and Jimmy
```

Tickets purchased at a party goods store were sold for admission to the various events. Tickets made from index cards were given out as win tickets.

Planning Attractions

The kids collected empty boxes discarded by their local supermarket. These were arranged in circular fashion around the yard and designated as booths housing the following activities:

1. Pick-a-Number

Supplies: large dish of water
Pieces of cork, each with a number pinned on the bottom
A small net of the type commonly used for scooping up goldfish

Procedure: The corks were floated in the water, and each customer scooped up a cork with the net.

Prize: If corks numbered 2 and 3 were scooped up the participant took another turn; corks numbered 4 and 5 resulted in a win ticket; and no prize was given if a child picked cork number 1.

2. Fishpond

Supplies: 2 boxes, piled one on top of the other
1 fish pole made from a stick and a string with a spring-type clothespin attached to one end of the string

Procedure: A carnival "employee" crouched behind the bottom box and attached a prize to the clothespin as the pole descended.

Prize: Every customer was a winner at this attraction.

3. Electronic Spin Artist Booth

Supplies: Dab-Art or Art-A-Matic battery-operated turntable purchased at a toyshop or department store
5"x7" white cards
Plastic bottles of red, yellow, blue, and black poster paint (liquid detergent was added to paint for easy removal from fingers and faces)
Old shirts to protect clothing

Procedure: Paint was dripped from the bottles onto a spinning card.

Prize: Every participant produced an artistic masterpiece.

4. Penny Pitch

Supplies: Empty dishes and pennies

Procedure: The player attempted to pitch 5 pennies into the dishes.

Prize: A penny in a dish close to the player earned one win ticket, and a longer toss landing in a dish earned two.

5. Tosseroo

Supplies: A large piece of white poster board with the following pattern drawn on it:

Game chips or pebbles

Procedure: The customer tossed 5 chips toward the card.

Prize: If a chip landed on A the player won one free turn at the fishpond, if it landed on C there was no prize, and if it landed on E the player could take another turn. Chips landing on B, D, and F earned the player a win ticket.

6. Makeup Booth

Supplies: Rouge, lipstick, eye makeup, and discarded jewelry, clothes, and hats

Procedure: Customers were made up and adorned as freckle-faced bums, red-nosed clowns, or blue-lidded dramatic actresses.

Refreshments

A carnival is not complete without eats. The children bagged homemade popcorn in waxed paper bags and sold it for ten cents. They put crushed ice in small paper cups and poured fruit punch concentrate over the ice to make snowcones. An ice bucket and all food was put outside to keep people from continually parading through the house.

Finances

A worthwhile side benefit of the carnival was the experience of handling money. The kids frequently stopped the show and counted their "take." The teen-ager put up capital for the purchase of tickets, refreshments, and miscellaneous items. He kept track of expenses and was reimbursed at the close of the successful event.

As the last child left, clutching a bedraggled stuffed elephant which he had won as a door prize, the youthful entrepreneurs made the final count. Bursting with pride and feelings of accomplishment, the three children ran into the house to report to their paint-splattered parents that they cleared $8.17.

Though drooping with exhaustion from the busy four days, the kids had enough energy left to argue about the extra penny.

The enterprising teen-ager had enough energy left to make a summer business of helping children in other neighborhoods organize their own carnivals.

Craft Activities

Some families keep a folder of simple ideas gleaned from magazines, newspapers, or craft shops and refer to it when children complain, "There's nothing to do." Others keep a record of projects the children initiate themselves but forget about as time passes.

The best ideas are those which require a minimum of parental preparation. One mother said, "I remember spending an hour carefully spreading newspaper on the kitchen table and placing several colors of paint in frozen-juice containers for my five-year-old Matisse. The child made three red strokes, two black, and and one green and announced, 'I'm done, Mommy.'"

"I wanted to cry," this woman added.

Below are several activities that occupy children's rather than parents' time and require no artistic talent.

Room Decorating

Any child over four appreciates freedom for self-expression in room decor. If possible, mount a bulletin board where the child can display posters, pictures, and treasured banners. Colorful posters can be made on large sheets of shelf paper.

Young children can decorate walls or bulletin boards

according to the season. For example, suggest that they cut out such things as pumpkin faces in the fall, snowmen with black buttons and carrot noses in the winter, and yellow daffodils in the spring.

A psychedelic room can be developed by teen-agers if they shine black lights on posters made with fluorescent paint.

Kids like to see life-size images of themselves on the wall. Draw the outline of the youngster's body on a large sheet of paper rolled out on the floor, and encourage the addition of eyes, ears, nose, mouth, clothing, and other details. When saved from year to year these figures show changes in growth and in self-concepts. They also make appropriate gifts when rolled up and mailed to faraway relatives.

Children enjoy creating their own wastebaskets. Keep a supply of round gallon ice-cream containers or cardboard cartons. These can be covered with construction or adhesive paper and decorated with sequins, buttons, or decals.

Sewing Activities

Keep a supply of scraps of material, yarn, and large needles on hand. The younger the child, the larger the needle should be.

Let children sew a paper bag shut or embroider on a paper plate. Have them either create the design with needle and thread as they proceed or draw it before embroidering.

Flat styrofoam containers used for meat packaging

are easily punctured with fat needles and yarn and when decorated can be used as wall hangings.

Iron-on initials and designs are available for kids who want to monogram a shirt, towel, or pillowcase or create their own patches to sew on jeans.

One child pleased her father on his birthday by embroidering a workshirt with a green frog on the back and the words "Daddy" and "pencils" over the pockets on the front. Her proud dad enjoyed the personalized garb as a conversation piece as well as an article of clothing.

Homemade Gifts

Before holidays and birthdays encourage children to make rather than buy gifts. A Florida grandma chuckles every time she looks at the daisied apron her granddaughter sewed for the bottle of detergent. Another reports that her grandson sent her a star-shaped piece of cardboard with pieces of succulent plants pinned on it. She and the child were equally excited when the plants on Grandma's star started to grow.

Family traditions can grow up around homemade gifts. One dad made a cannibal pin for his mother when he was in kindergarten. His folks saved this creature made from a halved cork, thumbtack eyes, and drapery hook earrings, and it goes back and forth across the United States on gift-giving occasions.

Here are some simple gifts which are easily created:

Spray-paint a block of wood which is approximately 5 by 3 inches. Nail a piece of leather cut from a discarded belt on the center of the block. Tuck flowers made from paper or straw into the strap.

23

Simulated stained glass can be made by scraping bits of crayon onto a piece of waxed paper. Place another piece of waxed paper on top and gently press the two pieces together with a warm iron.

Tissue paper moistened with liquid starch can be molded onto pop bottles to make attractive vases.

Glue pink tissue-paper cherry blossoms on a branch for a cherry tree any aunt or grandparent will cherish.

Make a towering toothpick sculpture beginning with a cardboard base and gluing picks together until a desired shape is reached. One fifth-grade boy kept his fragile statuary in his closet for two weeks before presenting it to his surprised and delighted parents on their anniversary.

Plant Hangers

Any youngster who can tie a knot will be thrilled with instant success when making these simple slings for hanging plants.

Using jute, plastic rope, heavy yarn, or string, cut 12 pieces, each 4 feet in length.

Tie one big knot in this group of strings, leaving an 8-inch tail at the end. Tie this tail around the leg of a table or chair so you can work on the floor.

Separate the strings into groups of 2.

About 8 inches down from the big knot, tie strings A and B together, then C and D, and so on until each group of 2 strings has a knot. Then pull strings A and L aside.

About 1 foot down from the first group of knots tie strings B and C together. Continue splitting strings off from their original groups and knot together strings *D* and *E*, *F* and *G*, *H* and *I*, *J* and *K*. Pull strings *A* and *L* over and knot them together at the same point that the other pairs of strings have been knotted.

Then move down to about 8 inches from the end of the cords and tie a loop for hanging. Invert the hanger and place a pot in it.

You can elaborate on this simple pattern by using several different colors of yarn and sliding beads to the knots.

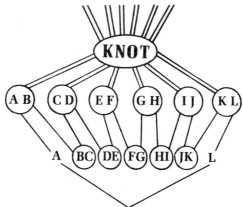

Mini-Masterpieces

Creative families never discard anything in the household without considering its potential.

One father, eyeing the whole skeleton left from a baked salmon, suggested that the kids place it under a piece of paper and rub over it with the flat side of a crayon. This amusing skeletal picture led to rubbings made from a variety of leaves and coins.

On another occasion this dad and his children made pencil dots on paper through the holes in the shaker top from an empty jar of garlic salt. Then they experimented with different patterns of dots.

Younger children are fascinated by the duplicates of their drawings produced with scraps of carbon paper.

Others like to ripple crayons over corrugated cardboard or draw on sandpaper with crayon or chalk.

Making a giant scribble and filling in the sections with vivid colors is another absorbing pastime.

Drawing around hands and decorating the paper fingers with glamorous rings and brightly colored finger nails amuses little people.

Toddlers can make Hawaiian leis by stringing empty toilet paper rolls.

Let budding artists preserve chalk pictures on colored paper by spraying them with hair spray. Instruct them on the proper use of aerosols, putting particular emphasis on spraying away from face or body.

A flattened cupcake paper makes an effective head for a circus lion or a body for a strutting turkey.

Miniature people can be made from the flat wooden spoons that come with individual ice cream sundaes. Draw faces on the "bowl" section and clothe the body with scraps of material. Wooden spoon families fit snugly into jewelry boxes.

Walnut shells lined with wads of cotton provide beds for even tinier dolls.

Cotton balls make fluffy clouds on children's drawings, and additional three-dimensional effects can be created with the styrofoam curlicues used in packaging.

Show youngsters how to make curly appendages for their animals or people by wrapping quarter-inch-width strips of construction paper tightly around the closed blades of scissors.

Bouncy legs for paper creatures can be made by taking two strips of paper of equal width and equal length, glueing them together at right angles, and folding them alternately one over the other. Glue again at the other end.

Creatures can be carved from potatoes or soap, or fashioned by fastening chunks of fruit, vegetables, or marshmallows together with toothpicks. Intriguing totem poles can be carved from carrots using knife or teeth.

A mother who bemoaned her lack of artistic talent said, "Even I could show my children how to make stick, heart, or circle creatures."

Inspired by her simple drawing, her children then created box and X people.

Art Box

A readily accessible art box is a must in any household where the words "There's nothing to do" are apt to be spoken. Keep adding new items to the box to maintain interest, and for special treats let the children use pinking shears or a stapler.

Basic items to be placed in the art box are: colored and white paper, pencils (with erasers), crayons, glue, scotch tape, blunt scissors. Other useful objects with artistic possibilities are listed below:

bit of aluminum foil	feathers
cellophane	bottle caps
egg cartons	jar lids for drawing
empty thread spools	circles
pipe cleaners	gummed star and stickers
ribbon	glitter
beads	ruler
bits of jewelry	paper punch

Many things that would ordinarily go into a trash basket take on fresh value when deposited in the art box.

Non-Craft Activities

Nature Projects

Bird-feeding will sometimes be a diversion for bored children. They can make food chains by stringing cranberries or popcorn and hang them on trees and bushes. They can scatter trails of broken crusts of bread, stale crackers, or cereal throughout the yard. Or they can make a simple feeder by covering a cardboard tube from a roll of toilet paper with a paste made of equal parts of flour and water. After the mixture has dried slightly, roll the tube in wild-bird seed. Hang it outside when thoroughly dry.

Children love to plant seeds, and those which sprout rapidly, such as radishes, corn, watermelons, pumpkins, beans, and sweet peas, are well suited for their garden. "Farming" activities satisfy an innate need for digging in dirt and help children learn to assume responsibility. They find out quickly that only plants properly cared for will live and produce vegetables, fruits, or flowers.

Toddlers delight in watching the growth that takes place when a carrot top or whole sweet potato is put in a dish of water. A family with grown children still count the curling vines of the sweet potato among their loveliest indoor plants.

An Indian Guide father showed his tribe of active boys how to make simple and inexpensive terrariums. In a 6- or 8-ounce clear plastic glass (commonly called Old Fashioned size), the boys layered the following: 2 tablespoons sponge rock; 1 tablespoon crushed charcoal (made by crushing a briquet with a hammer); 3 tablespoons potting soil. Two small plants such as Tiny Trailing Toad or Emerald Mound were planted in this mixture. The boys then added 1 tablespoon water and a decorative object, such as a redwood chip, a brightly colored marble, or a miniature statue.

They inverted another clear cup over the filled one and fastened the two together with cellophane tape. The terrariums grew well in a sunny place and no additional watering was required. The moisture which accumulated on the inside of the cups took care of the plants' needs.

An attractive indoor crystal garden can be made by children when they follow these steps: In a flat pie dish (glass or aluminum) or other shallow container pile pieces of wood, cork, sponge, charcoal, or broken pottery. Pour a solution made by combining 4 tablespoons noniodized table salt, 4 tablespoons liquid bluing, 4 tablespoons water, and 1 tablespoon ammonia over the porous pieces. "Look, Mom, my garden is growing," said an excited ten-year-old just one hour after he had placed his dish garden in a warm room.

Kitchen Experiments

Small fry can combine common food products to produce chemical reactions.

A mixture of baking soda and vinegar will result in a vigorous bubbly potion.

Dirty pennies that are dipped in a mixture of vinegar and salt will emerge shiny after they have been rubbed with a soft cloth.

Kitchen quiz games can be played by blindfolding children and exposing their senses to cinnamon sticks, pepper, cloves, a burnt match, or an assortment of extracts like peppermint or orange.

Melodious tunes can be played by tapping a spoon against the sides of glasses filled with varying amounts of water. Adding food coloring to the water gives visual beauty to this kitchen xylophone.

Toolbox Toys

The household toolbox is a mysterious wonder to most children. An improvised harp can be made by hammering nails into a block of wood and stretching rubber bands around pairs of nails at varying degrees of tautness.

Children enjoy making wire sculptures and adding nuts, bolts, and screws for interest.

They can make a magnet fish pole then explore their house for paper clips and bobby pins. If they put their accumulation of metal things in a box made of thin cardboard and run the magnet across the bottom they will have a traveling collection.

Simple Amusements

There is no plaything on the market superior to an empty cardboard box. It can become a car, train, raft, or sailing ship for an imaginative child. After a day of "sailing" in the carton which formerly held her family's new washing machine, a twelve-year-old girl remarked to her parents, "Kids don't really need toys."

A card table with a toy phone, a discarded checkbook, and pencils and paper on top is converted into an executive office. Placing a blanket over any table changes it into an instant tent.

At the end of a long summer, one mother and father balked at their children's demands for paid entertainment. On Saturday night they reached back into their memories for amusements from the "old days."

They took brown wrappers from candy boxes and showed the children how to blot out their teeth with the folded papers.

They totally darkened a room and cracked a white Lifesaver with a pair of pliers. Their kids were delighted with the green flash.

They rug-skated with the lids of shoe boxes, and they played hockey on roller skates. Jar lids and yardsticks became pucks and hockey sticks.

The *pièce de résistance* of that evening was the floating arm trick. The father stood in a 32-inch doorway. Letting both arms hang loosely away from his body he pressed the outside of his wrists (where the face of a watch is normally worn) against the door-jambs. While standing straight he pressed very hard, exerting pressure evenly against both wrists until his arms became very tired. This took about three minutes.

The father then stepped forward, with arms completely relaxed. His family watched in amazement as his arms floated magically into the air.

When a child with a probing mind questioned the "magic," he told her there is a tendency for the arms to lift because of the reaction of the tired muscles and the power of suggestion.

Other families recommend these activities, which sometimes keep their children busy for several hours:

Save gift catalogues which arrive in the mail and place them in a dream box. On boring days, or when birthdays are approaching, let the children initial items they'd like to own.

Balloons provide opportunities for children to use their imaginations. Buy long, skinny ones to be shaped and twisted into animals, Indian headdresses, mustaches, or walking canes. During the summer months children can have water fights with filled balloons.

In summer, too, runs through the spray from the garden hose or raucous hose fights will cool overheated children. Have them set up a plastic-bucket brigade and give them a lesson in pretend fire-fighting.

Children will often amuse themselves for hours when persuaded to clean out drawers. They will be surprised with long-forgotten paddle balls or birthday party trinkets.

Sometimes cleaning will lead to swap meets with neighbors. A woodburning set discarded by one twelve-year-old may become the prized possession of the boy next door.

One family with ample storage space saves all toys in good condition. When the cartons are produced on rainy days or at the end of summer vacation, even the thirteen-year-old is amused with the string of quacking ducks she pulled as a toddler.

Other families keep a surprise box for moments when there is absolutely nothing to do. This is filled with such things as fresh boxes of crayons, protractors, stamp pads, whistle rings, and packages of gingerbread mix.

A very patient mother and father keep television to a minimum in their home and do everything they can to prevent their children from plunking down for hours in front of the screen.

When their children are at a complete loss for

something to do, they suggest that the restless youths draw a picture or write a story about life with twenty-seven brothers and sisters, a house filled with birds and lions, or a flying bed.

In moments of sheer despair they heat a pot of water on the stove and tell their little ones to watch for a genie to appear in the steam.

Parties

One party-loving family says, "We use every possible excuse to have a celebration. We honored our three-year-old when he stopped sucking his thumb, our five-year-old when she learned to tie her shoes, and our nine-year-old when he successfully memorized the multiplication tables. We throw a party for contest winners, and for the first and last days of school as well as for outstanding report cards.

Birthday Celebrations

Eagerly anticipated birthdays are festive occasions in most families. A young mother describes celebrations which begin at breakfast with a candle in a cantaloupe, an apple, a muffin, or a doughnut. Birthday napkins are used at all meals that day, and the honored child wears a glittery crown. Favorite activities such as bowling, horseback riding, or miniature golfing are included in the day's plans.

An imaginative father suggests sending arriving birthday party guests on a hunt for sticks to sling across their shoulders. Wrap hobo lunches and party favors in red bandanna handkerchiefs, which are then tied to the sticks. A railroad car diner can be made from empty cardboard boxes.

A middle-aged couple who ran out of birthday party ideas for their five children now combine special occasions and entertainment funds and plan one big celebration a year for their kids.

In the yellow pages of their phone book, under the heading Party Planning Service, they found listings for magicians, clowns, puppeteers, ventriloquists, folk singers, mime and makeup artists, and balloon men with helium tanks.

College students who provide similar party entertainment, frequently at low cost, advertise on campus bulletin boards.

The library is a fresh source of ideas for ways to celebrate. One mother recalls, "I hated birthdays until we started patterning them after customs of different countries." This family began with a Swedish observance in which celebrants are awakened by their entire family and are never reprimanded, spanked, or criticized on their special day. They are allowed to stay up later than usual, to choose favorite foods, and to neglect their chores.

Halloween

"No holiday caused us greater anguish than Halloween," remarked the parents of two children in the primary grades.

The first year their children were in school they bought a tawdry princess costume for their daughter and used a tattered sheet for their son's transformation from boy to ghost. When they attended the annual Halloween parade at school they marveled as children in elaborate outfits ranging from ostriches to octopi marched by.

Here's how they costumed their children the following October.

During a cleaning spree the mother found loose garters from pre-pantyhose days and several nylons without mates. Her husband stuffed the stockings with tissue paper, and with the outmoded garters they fastened three stuffed stockings on the child's chest, three on her back, and one on each arm. They dubbed her an octopus.

They costumed the boy as a vampire, using black cloth for a cape, plastic monster teeth, and a thirty-nine-cent cardboard hat. For added effect they fastened green wiggly monsters on the flowing cloak.

As children get older they'll dream up their own ideas for costumes. A child out for an evening of trick or treat can masquerade as a bum, a peanut man, a suitcase, a balloon woman, a plant doctor, a frogman, an astronaut, or Miss America.

PART TWO

SUNDAYS

On Sunday each person or family must separately make what it can of the world.

—Charles A. Reich, *The Greening of America*

Mystery Car-Rides

As the pace of modern life accelerates, the need for relaxing Sundays becomes increasingly important. Children and parents return to their workaday world more refreshed after a day of rest than after a day of work.

One father who is employed six days a week said, "If we stay home Sunday afternoons, we are inundated with a myriad of C.L.J.'s, otherwise known as crummy little jobs."

To get away from work this family made a regular habit of taking a Mystery Car-Ride on Sundays. The joy of their drives was enhanced because only the parents knew the final destination. The sport of guessing was a major part of the day's fun, and even places visited many times before took on fresh appeal when transformed to an "MCR."

Occasionally one parent and one child would pick the secret destination, and the rest of the family did the speculating.

Here are some suggestions from the many families who have now made a tradition of the mystery car-ride.

Low-Cost Destinations

Drive to an airport to watch planes take off and land, to a dairy farm to watch cows being milked, or to a bakery to view pastry chefs decorating fancy cakes behind large glass windows.

Visit parks and play ball, feed the ducks, sail boats, throw frisbees, ride bikes, fly kites, or picnic.

Piggyback one mystery upon another by secretly arranging to meet friends at the park.

Drive to the store for the purchase of a game of Ring Toss or Pick Up Sticks, which the family can play together after returning home.

Never forget the simple pleasure of a drive to the ice cream store for a chocolate cone or foaming soda.

Seasonal MCR's

The changing seasons offer opportunities to plan outings to professional, college, high school, or Little League ball games.

Other seasonal sports are miniature golfing, ice skating, and fishing. In many states equipment for fishing and cooking the catch can be rented at privately stocked ponds.

Building sandcastles is a time-honored summertime treat.

Trips to roadside fruit stands for the season's first strawberries, corn on the cob, or Halloween pumpkins, surprise and delight most children. Apple farms welcome visitors in the fall and often feature a cider press in squishy action.

Educational MCR's

With a minimum of investigation families can find places to go that provide learning experiences for all. Visit a bird or wildlife sanctuary, arboretum, planetarium, or military base. Open houses at airports or fire stations are scheduled regularly in many communities.

Give children an opportunity to ride a train or bus if they've never been on one before.

Lecture series, local school presentations, and museum visits offer opportunities for cultural enrichment.

Special Events

One father and mother reminisce about a Sunday afternoon when they surprisingly came upon a dog show in a local park. The judging of the color, posture, and movement of the stately Irish setters was an unusual sight for the entire family. From that time on they watched for horse, flower, and art shows, and for antique auto exhibits.

Air events featuring glider pilots and sky divers performing daring stunts are thrilling experiences. Hot-air balloonists frequently do an on-site inflation and sell rides to eager customers.

Carnivals and fairs commonly pop up in shopping center parking lots on weekends.

Strawberry festivals, garden boutiques, and craft sales are fund-raisers planned by church-affiliated groups.

Finding New Places to Visit

One family keeps its address on the mailing lists of local colleges, art museums, science centers, and musical and theatrical groups. This way mystery car-ride ideas arrive by mail.

An organization devoted to the needs and interests of gifted children mails its monthly newsletter to anyone who pays the nominal annual dues. This is an excellent source of ideas for Sunday adventures.

The names of all kinds of community groups which feature activities for families are usually available from the chamber of commerce.

Local newspapers commonly list weekend entertainment. Pamphlets or postcards on racks in hotels and motels often reveal points of interest frequented by interested tourists. One family learned about a renowned old home in their area from a picture postcard. After several Sunday visits they became actively involved in its restoration.

Family Days

Some families prefer to spend Sunday afternoons and evenings at home with relatives and friends. The prospect of visitors is an incentive to plan activities which will make every Sunday a family holiday.

Icebreakers

Planning is important when company is expected. One hostess says, "If we'd invite another family without giving any thought to activities for the children, the younger ones would cling to their parents until fifteen minutes before departure and the teen-agers would sit and stare at each other across the room. We've developed ideas well suited to getting kids of all ages involved as soon as they get here."

This family plays cards, croquet, badminton, hopscotch, or Bingo. The older children sometimes hide peanuts and send the younger ones searching in flowerpots and tree stumps.

Ping-pong and darts tournaments are planned. Young children are supervised as they throw darts at inflated balloons.

The highlight of one family day was an art show patterned after a Parisian or Mexican bazaar. Paper and crayons were supplied, and when the children finished their pictures the adults strolled among the master-pieces and bargained for the art with pennies and sticks of gum.

Vast expanses of sidewalk can also serve as an artist's canvas with chalk used as the medium.

On another occasion the children were asked to paint abstract pictures and put their names on the back and an identification number on the front. The youngsters taped their pictures to the stonewall fence, and the adults judged Academy Award-style. Dramatically pulling a winning number from an envelope, they announced, "The winner is Hal, who drew this green and purple spiral design." Hal received a fresh drawing pad and crayons as a prize, and other entrants were awarded token prizes.

42

Games with Marbles

Games with marbles provide successful but low-cost family day entertainment, according to a New Jersey family.

They discovered an old African game called Kalaha, traditionally played by two people using pebbles and pits dug in the sand. This family made their own Kalaha set using styrofoam egg-cartons and marbles.

They removed the lid of the carton, cut the lid in half widthwise, and glued a section to each end of the carton to form two bins. Players sit with the egg carton between them and put three marbles in each of the six egg cups on their side.

The object of the game is to accumulate as many marbles as possible in the bin on one's right.

Kalaha is played as follows: Each player in turn picks up all the marbles in one of his own cups, starting from the left. One is dropped in each cup around the carton, moving counterclockwise, including, if there are enough, the player's own bin and the opponent's cups. A player never puts marbles in the opponent's bin.

If the last marble lands in a player's own bin, that player takes another turn. If the marble lands in an empty cup on a player's own side, that person captures the opponent's marbles in the cup opposite the empty cup and adds them to his own bin along with the capturing marble.

The game ends when all six cups on one side are empty. All the marbles left in the cups on the opposite side go into the bin of the player whose cups are empty. The winner is not necessarily the player whose side is empty, but the one whose bin contains the most marbles.

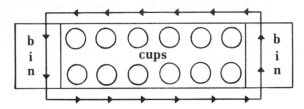

A *bare-foot marble game* is always a successful get-acquainted activity. Two flat dishes, one filled with marbles and one empty, are placed on the floor. Seated players try to pick up the marbles with their bare toes and transfer them from one dish to another. The winner is the player who successfully deposits the most marbles in the second dish within an allotted period of time. Several participants can be divided into teams and play the game as a relay.

Guessing Games

While players are still bare-footed from the marble games, line them up behind a suspended sheet or blanket. Let family members try to identify their children by their bare feet. This "feat" of identification is usually more difficult than it seems, especially if children are close in age.

A congenial *mind-reading party trick* is played as follows:

Line up nine books or magazines on the floor as shown:

One person, who knows the secret of the game, is sent out of the room. The remaining players agree upon one of the books as "it." The absent player is then called back into the room.

The leader, who also knows the secret, points to one of the books with a yardstick and asks the returning player, "Is it this one?"

The leader then continues pointing to other books in the group, asking the same question each time. To everyone's amazement, the guesser is able to identify "it"!

The secret of the trick is that the leader indicates the correct answer to the guesser with the very first point. The first time the leader asks, "Is this it?" the pointer is placed on a spot on the book that corresponds to the position of the book chosen as "it."

For example, if "it" is the book in the upper righthand corner of the group of nine, the leader points to the upper righthand corner of any of the books. This is illustrated by the dots in this diagram:

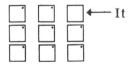

Discovering the secret sometimes takes a while. Players who think they know it take turns leaving the room and returning as guessers. If participants guess incorrectly they must join the group and play sleuth again.

Another guessing game in which some of the players know the secret is the *scissors game*.

Players are seated in a circle and a pair of scissors is passed from one person to the next. Players must, in turn, state how they received the scissors and how they passed them. For example, "I receive the scissors crossed and pass them uncrossed."

The object of the game is for all the players who don't know the code to figure it out. In spite of dramatic manipulation of the scissor blades by those who have played the game before, players not in on the secret must deduce that what those in the know are saying has nothing to do with what they are doing with the blades.

How one receives and passes the scissors is determined by the position of one's legs. A person with legs crossed may say, "I receive the scissors crossed." This player can then uncross his or her legs and say, "I pass them uncrossed."

Watching others' detective-like observations of the tricky scissors adds to the fun.

Paper and Pencil Games

Sundays can be used for teaching kids the games their parents played as children. Many of these, such as tic-tac-toe and Battleship, are packaged commercially, but they are just as much fun and far less expensive when played the old-fashioned way.

A favorite is Cootie, which is played with paper, pencil, and a die. Players roll the die, and if a 1 turns up, the body of the cootie is drawn. The rest of each person's cootie is drawn according to the following scale:

Throw Draw

1	body
2	head
3	eyes (2)
4	legs (16)
5	feelers (2)
6	tail

The first player to complete a cootie wins the game.

Writing Limericks

Another jolly activity, particularly well suited for parents and teen-agers, is limerick writing. The limerick can be a frivolous or sophisticated story in verse. Many are contained in books, while others are part of oral folklore.

To illustrate the meter and rhyme scheme read a limerick aloud to guests. This one was written by Edward Lear, "the Poet Laureate of the Limerick."

> There was an Old Man with a beard,
> Who said, "It is just as I feared!—
>   Two Owls and a Hen,
>   Four Larks and a Wren,
> Have all built their nests in my beard!"

The following homemade example may inspire would-be poets:

> There was once a young lady named Joan,
> Who was tired of staying at home.
>   She constructed a boat,
>   But the boat wouldn't float—
> Who has heard of a boat made of stone?

Some general rules for writing limericks are: the first, second, and fifth lines rhyme, and the third and fourth lines rhyme. Lines one, two, and five usually have eight or nine beats, and lines three and four have six beats.

To make a family game of limerick writing, supply each person with pencil and paper and allow time for thought. Then each participant writes a first line and passes the paper to the person on his or her right, who adds a second line. When the second line has been completed, the verse is again passed to the right for the addition of a third line. (Children too young to read or write can serve as "runners" passing papers from one poet to the next.) This passing continues until each person has written a fifth line, and then the limericks are read aloud.

Family Projects

There are mothers and fathers who find Sunday involvement in projects revitalizing and rewarding. "I never felt closer to my son than when we built a small kayak," said a father who spends many nights during the week out selling insurance.

"My children and I like to develop black and white photographs together," said a mother who is an art student. "We spend many happy Sunday afternoons in our tiny bathroom-turned-darkroom."

A divorced father who spent Sundays with his twelve-year-old daughter encountered a problem trying to simulate a normal family situation in his bachelor apartment. He could sense that a visit to a movie, restaurant, or other commercial attraction was no basis for building a father-daughter relationship. He knew the girl didn't particularly enjoy spending a day at his place, and he felt them drifting apart.

One day she said to him, "I'm sorry, Dad, but it's boring at your apartment. I'd rather stay in my own room and read magazines and listen to records."

Capitalizing on the girl's interest in country and western music, her dad suggested that they build a gutbucket. Together father and daughter began a search for the materials needed to build this simple percussion instrument. At a hardware store they found a galvanized washtub 19 inches in diameter. In addition they purchased 6 feet of plastic-covered clothesline, 1 eyebolt and washer, an eye screw, and a broomstick. As the curious clerk produced the cash register tape, he chuckled at his new role as gutbucket supplier.

Here are the steps this father and his daughter took to build the instrument:

1. Make a ¼-inch notch in the bottom of the broomstick and reinforce it with plastic or electri-

49

cal tape to prevent splitting. Rest the notch on the rim of the tub bottom.

2. Fasten the eye screw to the top of the broomstick.
3. With an electric drill, cut a hole slightly smaller than the threaded portion of the eyebolt, in the center of the tub bottom.
4. Insert the eyebolt through the hole and fasten with a washer on the inside of the tub.
5. Fasten the eye screw to the top of the broomstick, and tie one end of the rope through this screw.
6. Pull the rope taut, and, with the broomstick held vertically on the edge of the tub, tie the other end through the hole in the eyebolt.
7. Cut off the excess rope.

Demonstrating how to get music from a bucket, the father placed his right foot on its rim with enough pressure to hold it firmly to the floor. With his left hand he grasped both the rope and stick, pulling the rope taut against his chest while strumming with his right hand. He varied the resonant tones by sliding his left hand up and down to different positions on the rope and stick.

His girl was delighted with the plunking washtub music of the gutbucket.

The next Sunday they threw a western party and asked guests to bring guitars, banjos, brass, and recorders. Even wallflowers emerged to strum and hum during the successful jam session.

Father and daughter built additional gutbuckets to give as gifts, and through involvement in this project they achieved the closeness they sought.

PART THREE

SHIRK DAYS

Travel is one kind of experience that tends to feed imagination. The high spots linger long in our memories and strengthen our power of association—so much so, that years later, we may give birth to an idea that would not have come to us had we not gone somewhere and seen something.

—Alex F. Osborn, *Applied Imagination*

Organizational Guide
for Traveling Parents

Parents frequently become so involved in the child-rearing process that they forget the romantic charm of dinners alone or the luxury of uninterrupted conversations. Dedication to their task causes them to be reluctant to leave tots or teen-agers and to neglect the sparkle in their marriage.

One young mother and father recall that they had an opportunity to travel to Japan when their children were eleven, five, and two years old. "We agonized for a long time before friends convinced us that we'd never forget the experience and our children would not suffer permanent psychological damage from our absence. Having made the decision to go, we stifled our occasional guilt pangs and organized for our journey."

This couple developed the following plan, which can be used as a model for parents planning a trip without children.

Hiring Sitters

The first thing these parents did was look for a competent sitter. With grandparents and relatives thousands of miles away, they needed to find totally reliable substitutes.

After many phone calls and interviews they hired a woman with an excellent reputation for child care. She was willing to stay at their home, where the everyday surroundings would provide security for the children. The familiar faces of neighbors and friends might also provide a lift for a lonely tot.

To avoid the trauma of leaving the children with an adult they had never seen before, the sitter arrived a few evenings before the start of the trip.

The parents discussed their lists of instructions with her well in advance of departure to give her an opportunity to raise questions such as "Are the children allowed to stay overnight at a friend's house?" and "Do they like to be read to at bedtime?"

Lists, Lists, and More Lists

The Japan-bound couple provided as many answers as possible to any questions related to the smooth running of their household.

They compiled an emergency guide containing their home address (including the names of the nearest cross streets), and the names, phone numbers, and addresses of doctors, police, fire department, and hospital. Also included were the names and phone numbers of neighbors and close friends. They hung this framed guide by the telephone, and realized its everyday usefulness when their five-year-old told a delivery person the name of the cross street nearest their home.

Other vital information made available for the sitter and a neighbor was an itinerary of the trip, the name of the family lawyer, and the location of important documents . . . just in case.

They left forms granting permission for emergency treatment by the doctor or hospital personnel, and written permission for the children to ride in the sitter's car.

Their lists of the routine schedule of activities were designed to provide order and security in their children's lives. They felt that their absence was no excuse for their children to become sloppy in their habits or behavior. They hoped that beds would be made, clothes would be picked up, and eating would be confined to the kitchen.

They listed such things as bed- and nap times, usual mealtimes, and school, carpool, and bus schedules.

Vision of sedentary children watching TV for three weeks prompted this couple to list the amount of television normally allowed.

Other parents suggest that the following information be included in lists of instructions for sitters or grandparents:

Indicate the days for collection of trash and recyclable newspapers, bottles, and aluminum cans, and whose responsibility it is to get these items to the curb.

Provide for the care of plants. One mother neglected to inform her sitter that it was her ten-year-old's responsibility to water the houseplants. Because the sitter didn't know it, the greenery received double drinks and the results were catastrophic.

Avoid coming home to broken washing machines

and mountains of dirty laundry by leaving the names and numbers of dependable repair people. Authorize the sitter to call them in case of emergency.

Give careful thought to the children's needs and try to foresee every imaginable problem.

Anticipate stuffy noses and leave instructions for the administration of medication. Anticipate birthday party invitations and leave prewrapped gifts such as bubble bath or model airplanes.

Meal Planning

Food is another area of concern for departing parents. One mother returned from a trip to find that her chubby children had grown even chubbier. Learning that they had consumed too much cake and macaroni and cheese, she suggested nonfattening meals next time. She left cupboards stocked with low-calorie foods, and money designated for fruits and vegetables rather than cookies and candy.

A father was angered to learn that the sitter had forced his children to eat vegetables they didn't like. "The only accompaniments to entrees which they like are green salads, carrots, and applesauce," he said. "The next time we traveled we told the sitter not to bother buying or cooking spinach, green beans, or succotash."

Extra Preparations

Another couple, excited about their first trip to London, wanted to make it an educational experience for their children as well as themselves.

At the library they found books about London and its famous attractions, such as Westminster Abbey and the Tower. They read A. A. Milne's well-known poem "Buckingham Palace" to the children.

They discussed the difference in time and explained that while they were eating dinner the children would be sound asleep. "Piquing the children's curiosity produced unexpected side benefits," they said. While they were gone their sixth-grader's chart on time zones won an honorable mention in the school science fair.

They talked about traditional English food and bought kippers and mix for preparing Yorkshire pudding.

All these little extras helped parents and children feel a long-distance rapport despite the thousands of miles between them.

A Michigan family suggests that parents prepare a calendar for children, illustrating days in flight with a picture of an airplane and the day of their return with a red gummed star.

The parents purchased inexpensive surprises such as jacks and balls, toy baking sets, or balloons with cardboard paddle feet. Before they left, each lettered, wrapped item was put in a box and a letter placed on the children's calendar. On the day when B appeared they picked the corresponding gift from the box.

"This advance preparation causes the children to anticipate our departure rather than dread it," the father stated. "Eyeing the bulging box, they are more likely to ask, 'When are you leaving?' than 'Why can't you stay home?'"

Communication

Children need to understand that adults need trips with each other as well as with the entire family. They also need to hear repeatedly that their parents have confidence in them.

One mother and father think their final verbal communication with their sitter helps her and the children get along well with each other. Their parting words, within earshot of their children, are: "These are good kids, and we know you will have their full cooperation and respect."

Carefully planned written communication with youngsters is also important.

Parents plagued with a last-minute trip to the pediatrician were ready to get away from child care and responsibilities and relieved to be away at last. However, they smilingly recalled that during their first hour of flight they found themselves talking about their kids. Nevertheless, they were careful not to convey this instant loneliness in their letters.

To their seven-year-old they wrote cards about things to which she could relate. For example:

Dear Perri,

We visited Holland today. Count the number of red tulips that you see on this card. 1 5 4 9. We thought you would like this stamp with the queen's picture on it.

Love, Mom and Dad

And to the kindergartner they wrote:

Dear Hal,

The windmills are as big as the 🌳 in our front yard. They go around and around.

Love, Mom and Dad

This couple also arranged to receive mail from the children. They had learned a valuable lesson from a friend's unfortunate experience during her first trip to Europe: "I was gone three weeks, and each time I arrived at a new hotel I checked for mail. Finding none when I got to Switzerland, I burst into tears. Neither the snow-covered Alps nor the cheese fondue could take my mind off my children. I cut the trip short and scheduled an immediate flight home."

To prevent this total lack of communication with the home front, purchase aerograms at the post office and preaddress them. Indicate when the letter should be mailed in order to arrive on time and mark it "Hold for arrival."

Some children develop communication plans of their own too. Two girls look forward to their parents' trips and secretly tuck "We love you," and "Have fun" notes in their mom's and dad's luggage, hidden in pockets, shoes, and socks. These surprise love messages are very comforting to their parents.

Also comforting to traveling parents is the knowledge that they did everything they possibly could to ensure their children's physical and emotional well-being. Exhaustive pre-trip efforts add immeasurably to the pleasure of their journey and to the contentment of their children and sitter.

Family Trips by Car

"Some of our finest experiences as a family have taken place during carefully planned driving vacations," say a Dallas couple. "We laughed together, sang rounds together, and learned together.

"When we drove through gold country in northern California we read Mark Twain's short story 'The Celebrated Jumping Frog of Calaveras County.' When we visited Tempe, Arizona, we read a biography of Frank Lloyd Wright, who designed a desert-colored auditorium on the Arizona State College campus.

"We always left on trips with stacks of books and returned home considerably enriched."

They offer the following tips for planning a long journey by car.

Scheduling

When on a multi-day trip get on the road by about 5 A.M. Children under four will generally go back to sleep in the car until sunrise. As they get older they'll stay awake, and together families can watch the world of milk and produce trucks wake up and start rolling. Because of the light traffic during these early morning hours it is possible to cover about a hundred miles before breakfast.

Try picnic meals to break the monotony of long

driving days, and be prepared to deal with squabbling youngsters.

Trying Moments

For most families, the toughest hours of a day in the car are before lunch and at the end of the day's drive. The kids are tired and adult patience has worn thin.

For these desperate moments carry mystery packages. Simple items such as small balls for rolling, paper clips for stringing, and pipe cleaners for bending help the children settle down.

Another way to smooth rough spots in the day is to focus on the next stop. Think of a number and allow the child guessing closest to it to choose the restaurant for lunch. Or permit an accurate guesser to have the first choice of beds that night.

Putting kids on the lookout for a suitable motel, Grandma's street, or familiar landmarks sometimes relieves their boredom and turns their attention away from fighting with each other. Suggest that they pretend that they are pirates with telescopes, and give a token pirate treasure to the first child to spot the destination.

A popular treasure is a can of foot spray, which is a tickly refresher at the end of the day's drive. After removing shoes and socks, youthful travelers can spray each other's bared summer feet.

Survival Kits

A recently divorced mother who took her six- and eight-year-old youngsters to Yellowstone National Park said that her children bickered continuously during traveling time. "I neglected to plan for their day in the car, and my driving was dangerously distracted as the tension built. Fortunately we arrived safely."

Prior to her next trip this woman began accumulating travel survival kits. Instead of discarding shoe boxes, she filled them with empty paper bags for blowing up and popping, paper cups and twine for making telephones, and buttons for stringing.

She saved old purses and filled them with unused keys, powder puffs, small mirrors, collapsible plastic cups, and old family pictures. With an eyebrow pencil, the children would transform faces in these pictures into mustachioed kings and frowning clowns.

Before one trip she prepared a "direction" survival kit in which were tightly folded pieces of paper containing various commands. The children would reach in and pull out pieces of paper which instructed them to hold up four fingers, say the alphabet backwards, or count the cacti along the roadside.

A food kit is vital to survival when traveling with children. In addition to a vacuum bottle of water, take individual packages of cereal, raisins, and pretzels. Animal crackers provide entertainment as well as nourishment when children name the creatures that emerge from the box. And beef-jerky-eating children can pretend to be cowboys riding out on the range.

Other Ways to Pass Traveling Hours

A meticulous couple who take frequent automobile trips object to having bits and pieces of toys, games, and food cluttering the car. They came up with the following repertoire of travel entertainment using fingers and brains:

They would play imagination games about other cars on the road, such as speculating on what it would be like if everyone on the road were going to Grandma's.

They would wonder why a driver looked so sullen or another was smiling. They would see drivers bouncing their heads in time with music on the car radio and try to guess what song was being played.

They would call fingers into play and draw objects such as a ball, lollipop, or apple on a passenger's back. The person on whose back the picture was drawn would guess what object had been sketched.

The parents showed the kids how to make finger goggles for their eyes and would have them describe their sugar-coated dream castles as they looked through their magic glasses.

Or they would make earphones with their fingers and describe the sounds of roaring lions or oceans.

This family also developed the following group of "Royal Canadian Air Force" finger exercises, which are repeated ten times with each hand:

1. Spread the thumb away from the other four fingers.
2. Pull the pinkie away from its neighbors.
3. Put the pinkie finger and its closest neighbor together and pull them away from the index finger and its neighbor.

These exercises generally require concentration and some practice before small children can master them.

Other young tourists create faces on their fingers and

toes with a ballpoint pen. They plan puppet shows and dances for each other, or put their feet on the back ledge and entertain a make-believe audience. The smiling ink families always wash away in the bedtime bath.

A favorite trick for kids is sewing fingers together. They pretend to draw an imaginary needle and thread through the pinkie, then jerk it through the rest of the fingers until all the digits appear to be drawn together.

Another mother and father suggest these activities for the backseat contingent:

Carry several decks of cards in the car and teach the kids to shuffle. "That occupied our children's traveling time from Madison, Wisconsin, to St. Paul, Minnesota," the mother noted.

These parents also said that when on vacation they had more patience for teaching new card games. They purchased a book called *Fifty Card Games for Children*, by Vernon Quinn, from the United States Playing Card Co., Cincinnati, Ohio 45200. They never opened the book at home but found that without the distractions of telephone or television they always played new card games on trips. Learning the numbers and suits and sorting the cards provides excellent reading-readiness activity for preschool youngsters.

Take clipboards or similar firm writing surfaces for drawing on laps. A pencil, crayon, or felt-tip pen held very loosely on the surface of a piece of paper jiggles randomly according to the movement of the car to create "road pictures." Interesting designs result when driving on bumpy or curvy roads.

As the children grew older their parents provided duplicate maps on which they could follow the route.

Measuring distances and estimating driving time was a good way to reinforce math skills during the summer months.

During their drive to Washington, D.C., they marked memory spots on the map, and when they stopped in the evening they would record information about those spots in a trip diary. Rereading about awe-inspiring visits to the Smithsonian Institution and the Lincoln Memorial often proved more entertaining in later years than looking at photographs of famous places.

Photography

Picture taking is a vital part of any trip. A father and mother interested in photography advised their children to look out for scenes and lighting conditions that would contribute to a dramatic picture. Soon the kids were trained to see with the artistic eye of the photographer. They could spot edge lighting on a big green leaf or appreciate a diamond-like droplet of water on a lovely flower.

The parents emphasized words from the photographer's vocabulary, such as *vertical, horizontal, background,* and *foreground.* Together the family examined bark for its texture and sunlight for its shadows. They talked about seeing the order and beauty in nature: the lineup of kernels on an ear of corn or the ripples of sand at the edge of the sea.

In addition to learning to appreciate the elements in a pleasing picture the children developed patience with their folks, who often took a long time to set up a tripod or change lenses.

One of the most interesting things this family did

was to have the children use their inexpensive cameras to shoot scenes identical to those the adults shot. Their posttrip comparisons of photographs convinced them all that quality pictures are due to the talents of the photographer rather than the costliness of the camera.

Teen-Agers and Travel

As children's interests change they may become disagreeable about traveling with their families. A Pittsburgh couple disappointedly flew to Hawaii one summer with only one of their three children because the eighteen-year-old and sixteen-year-old were not allowed to take friends.

To avoid fragmenting families during vacations, some parents pursue new interests. "I'd never camped out until my twin boys left for college," said one mother. "But we still hoped to spend holidays and semester breaks together. After reading books on pitching tents and building campfires, we planned our first family camping trip. The boys remembered outdoor skills from Boy Scouts and enjoyed the restful break from pressured student days."

Another mom and dad who had never even slept outdoors decided to take a raft trip down a river with their high schoolers. Although they were apprehensive during their initial encounters with the icy rapids, by the end of the three-day journey they were inquiring about other river trips throughout the United States and Canada. Their teen-agers have willingly helped paint

65

the house and tend the yard to save money for additional adventures running the rapids.

This family's trip was organized by the American River Touring Association, 1016 Jackson St., Oakland, Calif. 94607. Information concerning many other tour operators can be obtained from travel agents.

Organizations such as Youth Systems Unlimited, Lake Tahoe Resort Hotel, P.O. Box 3566, Incline Village, Nevada 89450, involve young people in activities while their parents pursue adult entertainment. Weekend dances, Polynesian parties, or sports events are specifically planned for teen-agers who might otherwise grumble at traveling with Mom and Dad.

Opportunities for taking trips which will interest parents and teen-agers alike are endless, provided family members are open to new experiences. Vacations are available which revolve around backpacking, tennis, golf, or music. Many college alumni associations sponsor family camps, and summer family field studies are conducted by colleges and universities. Educational vacations offering classes in archaeology, natural sciences, and history are a growing trend.

Sending Children to Camp

A novel and needed switch occurs occasionally when children leave for camp and parents stay at home. "I get so tired driving my kids to bowling, sewing lessons, and the orthodontist," says one mother. "I couldn't survive the summer without that two-week break when they are at camp."

Children too need a break from parents and siblings.

Some youngsters balk at the idea of camp, even though they need an opportunity to develop independence and new relationships.

One mother recollects her experience with an obstinate son. To avoid a long period of apprehension, she didn't tell the child that she had enrolled him in a one-week camp session until three weeks before the departure date. The youngster cried when told, but after several family discussions seemed relieved that his parents had made this decision for him.

His mom and dad provided opportunities for him to bring fears about privacy, food, and unpleasant campers into the open. They talked about meeting children from families different from their own, and they expressed confidence in their son's ability to handle new situations.

This child wrote enthusiastic postcards from camp saying,

Dear Family,
   I'm having a really, really, really, really great time. I'm learning tennis and archery. Can I come for a month next year?

His parents saved the child's cards and letters, and each summer, when doubts began to creep into his mind, they revived pleasant memories with his bubbly cards and letters of years past.

A directory of over three thousand camps in the

United States, Canada, and abroad is published by the American Camping Association, Bradford Woods, Martinsville, Ind. 46151. The book contains information on camps featuring aquatics, canoe tripping, weight reduction, ecology, horseback riding, or programs with a spiritual emphasis. Camps with specially designed activities for physically and mentally retarded and disadvantaged children are also listed.

When One Parent Travels

It is not uncommon in the twentieth century for a man or woman to travel alone and leave behind one child who needs help with a report on electricity, another with a raging fever, a sink with a clogged drain, and a mate trying desperately to cope.

An adult in this predicament can choose to drag down the whole family's morale with endless complaints or send the mate off confident that the family members left at home will manage.

In fact, the absence of one parent can be an opportunity to discover anew how to have fun with the kids.

The single parent and children can plan exotic meals together, look at old photographs, experiment with makeup and hairstyles, or arrange a welcome home party for the traveler.

When one parent is absent from the dinner table, the other can concentrate on Jimmy's latest skateboard trick or Cindy's speech on crime prevention. Children welcome the undivided attention they crave but do not always get when the whole family dines together.

Evenings at home can be devoted to homework, woodwork, card games, or reading to children. "I feel very close to my children when my husband is away," says one mother. "We lend support to each other."

Adjusting to a mate's traveling isn't always easy. But the separation can be looked at as a gift of time that can benefit the children, the adults, and the marriage.

PART FOUR

WORKDAYS

Only a small part of education takes place in the classroom. . . . The family is a critical instrument in the transmission to children of values and motivation and the ability to accept responsibility.

> —Wilbur J. Cohen, *Innovator* (University of Michigan School of Education, March 10, 1975)

Making a House
Livable for Children

The importance of "home" in the lives of children and adults cannot be overemphasized. A house or apartment offers security, comfort, and a welcome refuge from the bustling world.

Within that refuge children need a spot which is their very own—a place where they can sulk or sing and muster their forces for coping with life.

Bedrooms

Children need a chair where they can curl up, a corner where they can hide, and a space where they can collect treasures.

"Our child's assortment of treasures caused a problem when we moved from our apartment," a young mother recalls. The boy had taped a sticker collection on his bedroom door and had to spend moving day cleaning the sticky residue.

After this family moved into their new home they installed a cork wall in each of their children's bedrooms. The twelve-by-twelve-inch squares, which cost approximately twenty-five cents each, were applied with linoleum paste and a metal spreader. The wall requires no upkeep and furnishes ample display area for newspaper clippings and honor certificates. In addition, it provides warmth, texture, and soundproofing.

Parting with accumulated treasures is sometimes difficult for children. One sixth-grade girl, tearful when her parents wanted to dispose of her four-year collection of letters and birthday cards, was given the choice of cleaning out her room and her clutter herself or having her parents do it instead.

Other parents allow a buffer period before throwing anything out. Favorite possessions such as torn and tattered lambs and lions are hidden, and if the raggedy friends are not missed after three or four months, they are discarded.

Kitchens

A mother who carefully selected desks, chairs, and lighting for her children's rooms laughingly says, "The kids do all of their school work and art projects at the kitchen table."

Children like to be where the action is, as noted by many parents who say, "We've got hundreds of square feet of house, and most of the time we're tripping over each other in the kitchen."

This hub of a family's activity is commonly a message center, work center, and play area combined.

A bulletin board mounted on a kitchen wall can hold work assignments, daily schedules, and meeting notices. Magnets can be used to convert refrigerator fronts to vital communication spots.

Children are always hunting for rubber bands for balsa gliders, and paper clips for school reports. Keep these items, as well as the stray buttons, washers, screws, and keys that accumulate in a home, handy in apothecary jars.

Pencils and scissors should be readily available, although a parent scrambling for a pencil near a telephone is a guaranteed occurrence in any household where children reside.

Large kitchen drawers can be reserved for empty coffee cans; empty egg, sour cream, cottage cheese, and yogurt cartons; and empty plastic medicine bottles. This drawer is baby's favorite and an older child's source of beetle and butterfly containers. Drawers filled with kitchen gadgets, such as a garlic press, a rolling pin, measuring spoons, and funnels, hold considerable fascination for growing children.

Bathrooms

Babies and their older brothers and sisters love to play in the bathtub. "We had a larger collection of toys in the bathroom than anywhere else in the house," said a father of three.

This family's supply, which hung in a plastic mesh bag over the tub faucet, contained empty detergent bottles, toy boats, meat basters, plastic medicine droppers, a discarded eggbeater, and toy dishes for bathtime tea parties.

Also available were rubber gloves with pinholes in

the fingers. When these were filled with water and placed over the faucet, children could pretend they were milking a cow.

Tub time can be used for washing pretend laundry. Supply a small washboard, string which reaches from faucet to soap dish, scraps of fabric, and toy clothespins. The first child in the tub can hang the laundry, and the second one can take it down and hang the next load.

Save soap scraps in empty cottage cheese cartons and teach children body finger-painting. Rub the scraps steadily on one area of the body until a heavy coating forms, then etch a picture with tapered fingernails.

Children who are expected to pick up dirty clothes and trash must be provided with clothes hampers and wastebaskets. One family suggests mounting wastebaskets on inside cupboard doors by placing two cup hooks on the inside of the door about half an inch beyond the sides of the receptacle. A screen-door spring or a length of chain can be attached to these hooks to form a sling for the wastebasket, which swings out when the door is opened.

Special adjustments need to be made for little people who cannot reach the medicine cabinet or have no drawer in which to put their toothbrush and cup. Plastic trays fastened to the inside of low cupboard doors accommodate these needs.

A child will spend hours looking into a mirror asking, "Who am I?" If the mirror is too high to find the answer, mount it on a door or wall and move it up as the child grows.

Household Tasks

"We do everything possible to make this home comfortable for our children," say a well-organized couple. "But they have to pull their weight too. There are certain jobs that need to be done, and the kids know we all work together to do them."

These parents frequently make deals with their children: "You mow the grass, and I'll have time to fix your bicycle." "You empty the dishwasher, and I'll have time to play a game of rummy." "Help me fold the laundry, and we'll have time to take a bike ride together."

"Making deals appeals to the children's sense of logic," the father adds. "For our family this technique works well."

Other families make games of household tasks. "We all hated to weed the yard," said one woman. "We decided each family member would be required to pull weeds for twenty minutes a day until the yard was neat and trim."

The children grumbled and complained about the assignment until it was turned into a weed-pulling contest. Each weeder was given a grocery bag and then picked an area of attack. The parents set the kitchen timer and gave a "go" signal. The kids dug in with gusto.

When the bell rang at the end of the contest, the father acted like a prize fight referee and made judging a suspenseful drama. The first prize was awarded to the child with the heaviest bag of weeds, and second prize went to the child with the next heaviest bag.

"The prizes were insignificant," their dad said, "but the drudgery of weeding became a little more palatable when treated as a contest."

Another way to assign jobs with a minimum of groaning from youngsters is to write various tasks on colored slips of paper which are placed in a hat, box, or bowl. Assignments can also be slipped into empty gelatin capsules (available at drugstores) and placed in a jar or dish. Each child picks a chore, and when finished, returns to choose another. Children cannot dispute the fairness of this method.

Orientation for Daily Living

Children learn many things by osmosis, but others need to be specifically taught.

"Shortly after we moved," said the mother of a three-year-old, "I asked our daughter to take a newspaper to Daddy in the back yard. When she went out the front door, I realized she needed orientation to the household." This mother and child toured the house daily naming bedroom, hall, closet, front door, and back door until the child knew what each was called.

Important Concepts

Children also need help with words like these:

top	bottom
big	little

under	over
fast	slow
above	below
right	left
walk	run
mine	yours
whole	half

One mother and father who cannot tolerate extreme noise in the home demonstrated loud and soft bangs with wooden spoons and pots. After this lesson in sound discrimination, they explained to their children that loud noises belong outside and soft ones inside.

The concept of time, which is extremely difficult for children to grasp, can be taught through frequent discussions of the terms *day, week,* and *month.* Explain them in relation to workdays, weekends, holidays, and birthdays. Help a child grasp the concept of a day by discussing sunrise, sunset, moon, stars, getting up, and going to bed.

If a child asks, "How long before we go to the store?" set a kitchen timer and depart when it rings. Or put the answer in terms which a child can relate to: "We will go to the store in the same number of minutes it takes you to eat your breakfast." Telling children when an event will occur (and sticking to that time line) will prevent the continual nagging question, "When are we leaving?"

Children should be taught to count from one to ten and the names of basic colors. One father and mother said, "No matter what we handed our daughter, it was always referred to as a yellow pencil, a blue napkin, or a red apple."

Teaching Preschoolers to Follow Directions

Learning to follow directions helps children function effectively at home and school. Simple commands such as the following will provide practice:

—Walk to the door, knock twice, and walk back to the starting place.

—Bring me three books and one pencil.

—Fold a piece of paper into four parts. Draw a blue circle in one part, a red circle in another, a yellow circle in the third, and a green circle in the fourth square.

—Turn off the kitchen light.

—Fill a cup half full of water.

Practice in following directions can be combined with exercises in memorizing. Give instructions which you ask the child to repeat before carrying out.

—Bring me two blocks.

—Bring me three green cars and five red wheels.

Increase the complexity of the commands until the child's limit is reached.

After children have learned the alphabet, instruct them to

—bring two objects that start with *b*

—bring two books with the letter *s* on the front

—find something with a *t* at the beginning of its name

When reading to children ask them to put a finger on the animal that starts with *c* or on the flower that starts with *r*.

Reading simple maps is another form of direction-following. Draw an area inside the house or out and send the child on a trip to various points illustrated with simple words or drawings.

All these activities will help equip preschoolers with reading readiness as well as the ability to follow directions.

Using the Telephone

No household device holds greater fascination for young children (and teen-agers) than the telephone. Instructions in how to use it properly should include telephone etiquette.

"When I found our three-year-old on the floor happily dialing and listening to the strange sounds coming out of the receiver," said a young mother," I isolated him in his room." This child soon understood the difference between the phone and his blocks and balls.

As soon as children are old enough to answer the phone they need to develop an awareness of the intonation of voices. Record their voices on tape or illustrate friendly and unfriendly sounds by speaking to them on the telephone.

Caution them to speak directly into the mouthpiece of the instrument and never to speak with food in their mouths.

"Please," "thank you," and "you're welcome" are vital phrases in anyone's telephone vocabulary.

Children need to be reminded to call people to the phone immediately. A father remembers that when he found the phone off the hook one day and picked it up to say hello, an angry caller on the other end reported that he had been waiting five minutes. A child had answered the ring and gone out to play without ever telling his father the call was for him.

Children should be told to hang up gently and to make sure the receiver is completely back on the hook.

Young people old enough to make their own calls can practice dialing with the receiver down. Once they know how to listen for dial tones and to take their finger all the way around the dial, let them practice by calling relatives or close friends. Instruct them how to act if they call a wrong number.

Children left alone should never tell strangers that their parents are not at home. In the case of prank or obscene calls they should hang up, or blow a whistle in the caller's ear. Insist that children write down messages for parents. One mother said, "My fifteen-year-old boy consistently forgot to give me news that friends had called." After this boy missed out on two parties and a trip to the beach because his mother purposely neglected to relay messages to *him*, he learned his lesson.

Children taking down information should repeat a name or number to be called.

Send children on a trip through the Yellow Pages, looking for amusements such as miniature golf or horseback riding. Teach them to find one Smith among a million by knowing initials or first names.

Help children develop listening skills by calling theaters and listening to the recorded announcements. Sometimes they need to listen carefully to the show-times of two or three movies before obtaining the desired information.

Keep an emergency guide of important numbers hanging on the wall near the telephone (see page 53 under Organizational Guide for Traveling Parents), and tell children they can ALWAYS dial 0 for help in any emergency.

Injuries and Illnesses

The word *emergency* needs to be carefully explained to young folks. "We had a daughter that yelled, 'Emergency,' every time she ran out of toothpaste, couldn't find a sock, or dropped a pin," said one dad. When this child cut her finger badly and no one came, she realized that overuse of this word could be dangerous.

Children are inclined to overemphasize their hurts. One father and mother recall when their daughter fell and hurt her ankle. The girl limped and complained for several days, but X rays revealed no damage; she just wanted to gain attention and annoy her family. They finally quieted her complaints by humoring her. All family members hopped around the house, and her ankle quickly healed.

Caring for children who are truly sick is not a humorous situation, but making games of illnesses sometimes helps.

One family whose five-year-old had a very sore throat could not force the child to gargle. As a last resort the mother, father, brother, and sister all gargled together in the bathroom. Amused at this strange-sounding quartet, the sick child finally joined in.

Sick children can be crowned king or queen of the day, with other family members serving as their court jesters.

An asthmatic child enjoyed getting in the shower with her mother and drawing hearts and choochoos on the steamy glass door. This relaxed the mother and relieved the child's clogged passages.

Children's Finances

Children can be stricken with inflation as well as with illness.

Methods of allowing a child to earn money vary. One mom and dad say, "We give our children an allowance in return for doing certain jobs around the house. If they find they need extra money we try to find more tasks for them." The children are not expected to pay club dues, charity donations, or entertainment expenses out of their allowances, which are for pocket money only.

Another parent says, "I got tired of doling out money all the time, so we discussed our fourteen-year-old's needs with him and established an allowance on that basis." If this boy doesn't have enough money left to go bowling at the end of the week, he stays home.

Some families give allowance raises on children's birthdays. Kids who need a raise in the middle of the year must submit a budget justifying the increase.

Another source of money for children is the refund offers that appear in newspapers and on bottles and cans of food and cleaning products. Children are willing to cut the brand name from plastic coffee can lids, soak labels from jars, or pry inner linings from bottle caps if it means money in the bank.

Taking children to a bank or savings and loan association provides an important lesson in economics. Most financial institutions will open an account with a one-dollar deposit. Patient personnel will tell young depositors about passbooks, quarterly interest payments, withdrawals, and newly minted coins. They will explain that the bank thanks people for the use of their money by paying them interest.

Preparation for Moving into the Outside World

Shopping Expeditions

Encourage children to take their own money with them when going on a shopping trip. Parents whose children ask for a new toy, six boxes of cereal, and every package of cookies in sight suggest that the youngsters finance the extravagance.

Taking children to the store can be trying and expensive unless ground rules are laid down. Some parents allow each child to choose one or two favorite items in addition to those on the grocery list. Others give the young shoppers coupons and let them gather those items. Children that cry and cajole will generally learn a lesson if left at home the next time.

Shopping can also be turned into a learning experience. Before leaving the house have each child make a list of four or five items with pictures or words. He or she can collect these items from low shelves while parents shop. Set a maximum budget for older children and instruct them not to exceed that amount.

The parents of a thirteen-year-old who still loves to go with them to the market have her plan an entire meal, check the pantry for ingredients, and shop accordingly. Preparing the meal also becomes her responsibility.

After the family returns home from the grocery store, young children can help by carrying tissues and toothpaste to bedrooms and bathrooms. They can wash and arrange fruit and fold up paper bags to be used to line trash baskets or wrap family lunches.

Respect for the Environment

Saving grocery bags is just one step in raising the environmental consciousness of children. One middle-aged woman says, "I used to laugh at my parents because they saved and reused aluminum foil and plastic wrap." Now that she realizes how important it is to protect the environment, this woman does the same thing.

Many families save old newspapers, bottles, and aluminum cans. "It would be so much easier to throw the glass away than to soak the labels off, store it, and transport it to the reclamation center," says one father. "But I felt a responsibility to set an example for my kids."

Members of another family frequently review the things they can do to save energy. With reminders to turn off lights, to turn off the shower water when sudsing hair, and to avoid letting the water run when brushing teeth, they are all more careful.

Collecting pull-top rings from cold-drink cans became a habit with a western family when their children learned that the aluminum rings were recyclable. Realizing it would take a long time to collect enough aluminum to turn in, they decided to string the rings and see if they could reach a thousand. Rings are strung in groups of tens and hundreds, and the children's counting skills have benefited as well as the environment. They have become compulsive about collecting rings at the beach, at ballgames, or when camping.

Safety and Self-Defense

Unfortunately the environment is sometimes hostile, and efforts to teach children about safety and self-defense are being intensified.

One couple who lived in an isolated area related that their fifteen-year-old daughter panicked whenever they left her home alone at night. She would stay awake hearing imaginary noises and worked herself into a frenzy at the slightest sound. After the parents returned late several times and found their daughter still awake, they decided to do something.

Together mother and daughter enrolled in a self-defense class where they learned tactics that would help them and the men in their family to defend themselves in any threatening situation.

In any potentially dangerous situation, children should be encouraged to observe the following rules.

1. Be aware of everything going on around you.
2. Evaluate the situation.
3. Keep calm.
4. Distract the attacker by doing something— anything that might work.
5. Watch for split-second opportunities and run!

Blood-curdling cries or screams such as Indian war whoops or karate yells like "Keeyi" or "Sato" suggest strength and power and might frighten an attacker away. A child's yell of "Fire!" will draw more attention than a cry of "Help!"

Self-defense experts suggest that children who walk to school alone in the dark or return from sports events at night should carry a piercing whistle which can be purchased at any sporting goods store.

Another item that fits in hand, purse, or night table drawer is an S.O.S. buzzer. This battery-operated alarm makes an earsplitting sound when its tiny pin is pulled. A more expensive variety also features a flashlight.

Children need not be filled with fear of an attack, but they should be prepared with appropriate responses in case they are faced with danger.

Filling Out Forms

The many things children need to know as they move from the world of home to the world of school and related activities are frequently overlooked.

A father shares this story of an oversight which became apparent when he took his ten-year-old boy to the bowling alley to sign up for Junior League. "The director handed Joe a card to fill out. The boy didn't notice that his last name was supposed to come first, and he didn't know how to write the date in numerals to fit in the too small space provided. The child's frustration grew as he struggled with the spelling of the neighbor's last name asked for 'in case of emergency.'"

As this father helped his son with the form he tried to think of other vital information the youngster might need to know. When they returned home he typed the following items on a card, and his son practiced filling in the information until he could do so with ease:

Name _____ Date_____
       Last   First Middle

Address _____ Age _____
      Number Street

_____ Birthdate _____
      City   State Zip

Home Phone Number_____ Grade in School____

Father's Name _____ Mother's Name_____

Father's Occupation _____ Business Address _____

Mother's Occupation _____ Business Address _____

Doctor's Name _____

Doctor's Address _____

Local person to contact in case of emergency

Neighbor _____ Phone _____

Friend or Relative _____ Phone _____

Giving children practice in filling out forms of this nature might protect them from confidence-shattering experiences at a later date.

Encouraging Learning

"The most difficult problem we have yet encountered as parents," say a concerned couple, "has been helping Tom, age eight, learn to read. Aside from feeling a sadness for this child who protested, 'I hate to read,' we could foresee insurmountable school difficulties if he didn't have a change in attitude.

"We knew he was bright, that his vision was perfect, and that he enjoyed books when others read to him. The problem was in the material he was capable of reading.

"'I want to read stories like Lisa,' he'd tell us. We couldn't make him understand that he had to be able to handle simple books before he could read the more complex material that his older sister devoured."

This family spent many painstaking hours dreaming up tactics to help their boy develop a positive attitude toward reading. The following are some of the methods they used to solve their important problem.

Labels

They labeled household items. Everything in the house had a sign on it—"green plant," "big window," "little chair," "front door," etc. Using a label-maker, their daughter marked items like toothbrush, closet, light switch, and clothes hamper.

To add interest to the game they would mark items incorrectly and ask Tom to find the errors. The label "toilet" would be placed on the telephone, or "candy" on a can of dog food. If Tom made the corrections he was rewarded with high praise.

Sometimes the family would put messages on each other's back. If Lisa laughingly put a sign on her dad that read, "There is a giant behind you," Tom would come running to read the sign.

Placing small objects on marked cards was another reading game. If Tom could put a dime, an apple, and a stick of gum on the appropriate word he was allowed to keep the goody. As he grew comfortable with this, the number of objects was increased to five, seven, or ten.

Note-Writing

When Tom tired of the labeling games, the family began an intricate system of note-writing. He called his parents "the mad note-writers," but read their messages nevertheless. Once he found a jumping bean taped to a piece of paper in his school lunch with the message "Don't eat me." They put notes under his plate at mealtime, on his pillow at bedtime, and on the faucets at bathtime.

Tom's attitude toward reading improved, and he was progressing nicely in school. Still his parents felt the need to keep up his interest with some consistent method.

One day during the summer, when the kids were asking questions about picnics, orthodontist appointments, and meals, their mother hit on an idea which would keep them informed about family activities and also keep Tom reading during the summer months.

The Daily Schedule

Tom and Lisa's mother began writing daily schedules which she placed on the refrigerator door with red ladybug magnets.

Thursday

Today we'll be flexible.

Breakfast: apple juice, cereal, poached eggs on toast, milk.

No fighting today, please.

After lunch we will go shopping. Make a list of five foods you would like to buy. You may choose one treat.

Will it be chocolate?

After dinner you may watch television.

Tom, if you read this schedule out loud you may stay up until nine o'clock.

Variations were made in the daily schedule by replacing some words with pictures. For example:

Friday

Happy Birthday, Tom. What kind of would you like?

Before your party we must take Lisa to have her fixed.

Sometimes blanks were left for the children to complete. Tom filled in the blanks made with red pencil, and Lisa the blue. This variation helped spelling skills also.

Saturday

Hooray! Dad is hom__ today.

Do you think he will use his ha__er or screwdrive__?

Lisa, where would you like to go today? _____

How about you, Tom? _____

The daily schedule was based on a system of tangible yet simple rewards, such as choosing the main course for dinner or the spot for a family picnic. Other times it might be designed like a ballot:

Sunday

Vote for the thing you would like to do today.

	Tom	Lisa
Go to the beach.	☐	☐

	Tom	Lisa
Go bicycle riding.	☐	☐
Read a book.	☐	☐
Have a family picnic.	☐	☐
Go bowling.	☐	☐

Be sure your X goes inside the box.

"Tom never voted for reading a book," says his dad; "and when he began third grade we still read to him at bedtime. Lisa often joined us, and we tried to make this a very special time for the children.

"We'd discuss how they felt about the story and give them opportunities to make up new endings. We talked about the pictures words made, such as bright orange, zooming rockets. We did everything we could to show Tom the pleasure a person can get from books.

"Then we discovered the 'cliff-hanger' technique. We would read to him and stop in the middle of an exciting part of the story. In spite of protests we'd kiss him good night and leave the room. To his questions of 'May I stay up and read?' we'd always answer, 'Yes.'"

The parents of nine-year-old Josie were concerned about her lack of interest in leisure-time reading. The child was always asking questions, however, and her parents secretly recorded these in a notebook. Then they surprised Josie with her very own book of "How Comes?" and a set of reference books geared to her age level.

Josie's reading career was launched as she began to seek answers to some of the following questions:

—How come witches always have big chins?

—How come tree bark looks like pieces of a puzzle?

—How come peanuts grow in shells?

—How come I can't go back to sleep and continue my dreams?

—How come my brother always wants the prize in the cereal box?

—How come grown-ups like anchovies?

—How come you don't spell "fun" with a *ph*?

Home Vocabo

Words are a major interest for another family, and by making adaptations on the game of Bingo, they have established an enriching home activity.

"Playing Vocabo requires a constant tuning in to words," states the mother.

Each time a member of this family asks the meaning of a word, someone looks it up and designates it "word for the week." It is written on a large chart kept on a bulletin board in the family room. Definitions are put on cards and stored in a file box.

When they play Vocabo each school-age child receives a sheet of paper divided into squares which are large enough to accommodate a beginner's scrawl.

The kids select words from the chart on the bulletin board and write one in each square. As a parent reads the definitions the children cover the appropriate space with a button.

Prizes are given for covering a row or an entire sheet, as in Bingo, and each child has a fair chance because winning depends on the random selection of words from the chart as well as on knowledge of the definition.

The repetition and constant use of Vocabo words has helped these children assimilate them into their vocabulary, and their parents hear the fourth-grader using words like *fiasco* and *obstreperous* just as casually as she uses *cookie* or *bicycle*.

Friends of the family remarked about the Vocabo game, "Once we walked into their house and their chart was not up on the bulletin board. We missed it, because we enjoyed the challenge of defining the latest batch of words."

Another family began playing Vocabo at home, and after their kids grew up and went to college they would still find themselves saying, "That's the word for the week," when an unfamiliar term popped up in their daily conversation.

The Metric System

The Vocabo game is also a convenient way of teaching the metric system. "We're going to ease the transition by educating everyone at home," says a middle-aged father.

Members of this family learned the base words, *meter*, *gram*, and *second*, and players write the following prefixes on the "Bingo" sheet:

mega	1 000 000	deci	.1
kilo	1 000	centi	.01
hecto	100	milli	.001
deca	10	micro	.000 001

One person calls the number and the players cover the appropriate prefix.

Conversion factors might also be called; for example, if a player has 2.54 centimeters on the paper, he covers it when the caller says, "One inch."

Other families have adapted this game to music and art appreciation. One woman confessed, "I never had much exposure to art and have always felt inadequate when visiting museums."

Too embarrassed to make uneducated comments about her artistic tastes, this woman is now trying to learn about art and help her children feel comfortable with it at the same time. She goes to the local library and checks out art prints and books related to the same artist. After her family has studied several artists, they play a game similar to Vocabo, substituting facts for word definitions. For example:

"This is a living American artist who paints gray-brown landscapes and weathered wood shacks in Chadds Ford, Pennsylvania, and Cushing, Maine."

The players cover the name Andrew Wyeth.

The activities of these families illustrate the endless possibilities for creative learning which the Bingo concept allows. And, of course, encouraging learning at home has carry-over effects at school.

The Public Library

Frequent visits to the library play a vital part in a child's attitudes toward books and learning.

Most librarians are eager to help children select books or to show them how to use the card catalogue.

They will also provide parents and children with information about the Newbery and Caldecott Award-winning books.

Trips to the library for books or for participation in summer reading programs and story hours should be leisurely rather than hurried stops at the end of a long string of errands.

One family keeps a file bulging with lists of recommended children's books clipped from magazines and newspapers. "Hi-Low books (high interest, low vocabulary) were the first books my child was interested in, and I learned about them from a magazine article," says a young mother.

A father whose child disliked going to the library picked books from different sections such as biography, science fiction, history, funny stories, and mysteries each time he went. "The books that finally stirred my television addict's interest in the library were those suggesting ways for children to earn money," this father said.

The library offers some of the best entertainment in a child's world. And it's free.

PART FIVE

FEEDING TIMES

In thinking up what to cook and how to cook it—in
thinking up new ingredients and new shapes—in every
aspect, cooking can challenge imagination.

—Alex F. Osborn, *Applied Imagination*

Do-It-Yourself Favorites

Kitchen activities provide stimulating learning experiences for boys and girls. Eyes open wide the first time they see apples become sauce, rice absorb moisture, or bread dough rise. Cooking brings together skills in science, reading, and math, and it helps youngsters develop an awareness of smells and tastes.

Children who can prepare a nourishing and appetizing meal are an invaluable help to working mothers and fathers.

Experienced parents recommend, however, that young people who cook must be bombarded with the message GOOD COOKS ALWAYS CLEAN UP THE KITCHEN.

Here are some suggestions for foods which very young children can easily prepare without the use of heat.

Homemade Butter

"Whenever I buy whipping cream, the kids quickly ask to make butter," says a mother of three active boys. They vigorously shake the cream in tightly covered plastic containers until rewarded with creamy sweet butter.

Experimental Salad Dressing

Youngsters who do not like vegetables may be enticed to eat several helpings of salad if they fix this oil and vinegar favorite. The ingredients in this dressing do unexpected things.

1½ cups oil
⅓ cup vinegar
1 teaspoon sugar (or equivalent amount of artificial sweetener)
1½ teaspoons salt
½ teaspoon dry mustard
4 cloves garlic, crushed in a press

Tell the chefs to observe how the oil and vinegar separate and to watch the salt go to the bottom and send up bubbles which burst on the surface. Let them watch the garlic sink to the bottom of the jar.

Add appeal to green salads with sunflower seeds, walnuts, toasted slivered almonds, capers, or croutons which kids can make from toast.

Cookie and Cake Decorating

Buy refrigerated cookie dough or large packaged sugar cookies for young artists to decorate. Stock frosting ingredients or canned frosting, silver balls, colorful sprinkles, and tubes of glossy decorating gel.

A simple train cake can be made by cutting a loaf or flat cake into several rectangles that resemble train cars. Supply dishes of colored frosting, Lifesaver wheels, and short peppermint-stick hitches. Colored sprinkles, coconut, and thin licorice ladders complete this easily created masterpiece.

Sparkling Fruit

Supply kids with apples, plums, pears, and grapes which they dip into a mixture of ½ tablespoon water and 1 egg white. Let the excess coating drip off the fruit, then roll it in extra fine granulated sugar. Set it to dry on paper towels until a glittery crust forms.

Peanut Butter Balls

According to a family of evening snackers, "A plate of these delectable cookies disappear from our refrigerator within an hour." This is a simple but nourishing treat.

½ cup peanut butter
½ cup honey
1 cup instant nonfat dry milk
½ cup Rice Krispies, coarsely crushed

Combine all the ingredients, then roll the mixture into balls and refrigerate.

The following recipes require baking or cooking, but young children can aid in the food preparation:

Pigs in a Blanket

Children will be heaped with praise for their culinary talents when they pass this dish to family or guests. Spread out the dough from a tube of refrigerated crescent rolls and separate at the perforations. Cut each triangle in two and wrap the dough around cocktail franks, or regular-size hot dogs which have been cut in thirds. Follow the baking directions on the package of rolls. Serve with mustard for dipping.

Pancakes

Children love to watch butter sizzle in the pan, to name the animal shapes created by the flowing batter, and to flip the puffy hot cakes. If necessary kids should stand on a chair or stepstool to be at a proper working level in relationship to the frying pan.

Freeze double batches or leftover amounts of pancake batter in empty paper milk-cartons.

Toasted Pumpkin Seeds

Any child that ever carved a jack-o'-lantern loves to run his fingers through the slippery seeds. After this mushy experience spread the pumpkin seeds on a cookie sheet to dry, then follow the directions below for making a tasty, toasty snack.

Preheat the oven to 250°. Put 2 cupfuls of seeds in a shallow metal baking pan and sprinkle with 2 tablespoons melted butter and 1 teaspoon salt. Bake for about 15 minutes or until lightly browned. Stir occasionally during baking.

Other seasonings, such as 1 teaspoon garlic salt or Krazy Mixed-Up salt, can be substituted for the plain salt.

Nuts and Bolts

Another snack which kids can make to eat or to give as gifts is made as follows:

1 package Rice Chex
1 package Wheat Chex
1 package Cheerios
1 bag fine pretzel sticks
1 pound nuts
1 pound butter

Preheat the oven to 250°. Combine all the ingredients in a large, flat pan and pour melted butter over the mixture. Add salt to taste and stir thoroughly. Bake 2½ hours, stirring every 15 or 20 minutes.

Homemade Granola

This mouthwatering cereal-snack is delicious plain, or as a topping on yogurt or ice cream.

8 cups uncooked oatmeal
2 cups shredded coconut
2 cups wheat germ
2 cups brown sugar
¼ cup water
1½ cups cooking oil.

Preheat the oven to 200°. Combine water and oil then blend into the dry ingredients. Spread the mixture in large baking pans or glass baking dishes. Bake 2 hours, or until golden brown, stirring frequently. Add 2 tablespoons vanilla after removing the cereal from the oven. Store in tightly covered containers in the refrigerator.

Gelatin Desserts

Making gelatin is as significant to children's food experimentation as taking steps is to their physical development. They are fascinated with the liquid's change to a solid and with the bright colors. Let them experience the taste of the smooth, cooled liquid, then pour it into aluminum foil muffin cups, fancy-shaped molds, or custard cups. Float marshmallow clouds on top.

Magic gelatin which will not melt at room temperature, can be eaten like candy, and makes a hilarious hit in school lunches is prepared as follows:

Combine 1 6-ounce package and 1 3-ounce package of regular gelatin dessert, 4 packages of unflavored gelatin, and 4 cups of boiling water. Put in a large flat pan or dish and cut in cubes when thoroughly chilled.

Low-calorie gelatin dessert can be substituted for the 9 ounces of regular fruit-flavored gelatin.

Barbecue Desserts

Banana boats are a favorite of camping families, Girl Scouts, and backyard diners. Split each banana, leaving

105

the skin on. Fill the slit with chocolate chips and miniature marshmallows. Wrap the bananas individually in foil and heat over a fire.

Smores are made from a sandwich of graham crackers, with a chocolate bar and marshmallow cream filling. They too are individually wrapped in aluminum foil and heated.

Roasting marshmallows is an ageless tradition. Have children hunt for long sticks or unbend coat hangers to use as cooking implements. A marshmallow can be roasted and eaten layer by succulent, crisp layer until nothing is left.

Clingy Clam Balls

This high-protein recipe surprises children because of the way the dough clings together and because of its mysterious green color.

1 8-ounce can minced clams
½ cup butter or margarine
½ teaspoon poultry seasoning
¼ teaspoon salt
1 cup flour
4 eggs

Preheat the oven to 350°. Drain the clams and add water to juice to make 1 cup. In a saucepan, combine this liquid with the butter and seasonings. Heat to boiling, then add the flour and cook until the mixture clings into a ball. Remove from heat. Add the eggs, one at a time, beating well after each addition. Stir in the drained clams. Drop teaspoonfuls of the mixture onto a greased cookie sheet. Bake 10 minutes and serve hot.

Fondue Bourguignonne

This relaxing main-dish recipe calls for each diner to participate in the cooking. A fondue pot or deep fryer is placed in the center of the dining table and one-third filled with salad or peanut oil heated to deep-frying temperature.

Provide each person with 6 to 10 ounces of steak cut in cubes, and an insulated fondue fork for COOKING PURPOSES ONLY. After cooking the meat in the hot oil, remove it to the dinner plate to be eaten with a regular table fork. Diners not following this procedure will burn their mouths.

Simple sauces such as horseradish, curry, thousand island, mustard, or green garlic, and condiments such as chopped boiled egg, peanuts, green pepper, onion, chutney, or chunks of fresh or canned pineapple, will be gobbled up along with the savory meat.

Sauces can be bought ready bottled, made from packaged mixes, or prepared from scratch like this green garlic sauce recipe:

2 cups mayonnaise
¼ cup salad oil
¼ cup lemon juice
1 clove crushed garlic
1 teaspoon dill weed
1 teaspoon paprika

1 teaspoon Maggi seasoning
salt to taste

Combine all the ingredients and add a few drops of green food coloring.

Dessert Fondue

Dipping chunks of sponge or pound cake, or fruit, in a sweet sauce is a fondue finale for a special meal. Brush slices of apples, bananas, and pears with lemon juice to prevent darkening. Melt the following dip ingredients in a small fondue or baking dish and continue to heat gently:

12 ounces chocolate chips
½ cup sugar
1 tablespoon butter or margarine
1 cup eggnog or cream
1 teaspoon vanilla

Just stir and dip.

Production Line Recipes

Even though kitchen experiences are important for children's growth and development, many adults don't appreciate having little people in the kitchen.

One busy mother says, "I have three children, who

all like to prepare food. If I let one help, the other two fret. And frankly I can't stand being in the kitchen with all three of them underfoot."

This woman solved the problem by developing production line recipes. She lines up the ingredients, shows the children what to do, then leaves the kitchen. They have more fun when they are not being scolded every time they drop a crumb on the floor.

The kids draw straws for the first job, then set a kitchen timer for fifteen minutes. At the end of the period they switch tasks and then set the timer again until each child has had a turn at each step of the recipe. "No one complains about favoritism," this mother reports.

The following are some of her special child-oriented recipes:

Turkey Sandwiches

Line up the following items on the kitchen counter:

1 dozen hamburger buns or French rolls
1 pound thinly sliced Mozzarella cheese
1 pound cooked, sliced turkey.

The butter mixture is made by adding the following ingredients to ½ cup softened butter:

¼ cup minced onion
½ teaspoon prepared mustard
1 teaspoon poppy seed

The first child in the production line butters the top halves of the bun or roll. The next chef puts a slice of turkey and a slice of cheese on the bottom of the bun and puts the two halves together. Number three cook wraps the sandwiches in aluminum foil. Bake the sandwiches at 350° for 25 minutes, or freeze in foil then heat 45 minutes when ready to use.

Crunchy Chicken

Wash a 2½- or 3-pound chicken which has been cut up. Using a rolling pin on waxed paper have one child crush 3 cups of Rice Krispies or potato chips. The next child can dip the chicken in ½ cup salad oil, and a third can roll the chicken in the crushed coating. Place the chicken in a shallow pan and bake in a 350° oven for 1 hour.

Cheese Balls

Provide bowls and flat graters and have the kids grate ½ pound of Cheddar cheese. To the grated cheese add the following:

1 cup flour
1 teaspoon salt
½ cup butter or margarine

Children can take turns kneading the mixture and shaping it into marble-size balls. Put on an ungreased cookie sheet and bake in a 350° oven for 10 minutes.

The cheese mixture can be wrapped around stuffed

green olives if desired. It can also be frozen in a large chunk and made into small balls at a later date.

Cheese Fingers

This is an appetizing way to use slightly stale bread.

8-ounce jar of sharp cheese spread
½ pound butter or margarine
1½ loaves of sliced white bread

Have the ingredients at room temperature. Mash the cheese and butter together.

The first child in the production line can cut the crusts off the bread, the second flattens the slices of bread with a rolling pin, the third spreads the cheese and butter mixture on the flattened bread, and the last one rolls each slice tightly like a jelly roll.

Place the cheese fingers on a greased cookie sheet and bake in a 350° oven for 30 minutes. (Save the crusts for feeding the birds or freeze until the next trip to a duck pond.)

Peanut Butter Cookies

This huge recipe will keep kids busy for hours. They might need a bit of adult assistance with the stiff dough.

1 cup brown sugar
1 cup white sugar
1 cup butter or margarine

2 eggs
1 cup peanut butter
3 cups flour
2 teaspoons baking soda

Cream the sugar and butter. Add the eggs and peanut butter, then sift in the dry ingredients.

Two children can roll the dough into 1-inch balls which they place on a greased baking sheet. Using a fork dipped in cold water, the third child flattens the balls into cookies. Bake in a 350° oven for 12 to 15 minutes or until browned.

Using Leftovers

Using leftovers is a challenge to any cook's creativity. Here are some suggestions for sneaking leftovers into appealing foods.

Add leftover party dips to chicken, turkey, or tuna salad, or use them as sandwich spread.

Store potato chip crumbs in tightly sealed containers for use as casserole toppings. Stale bread, crumbed in a blender and stored in the refrigerator, will serve the same purpose.

A whimsical father suggests combining small amounts of leftover juice (which take up precious refrigerator space) and telling children the mixture is a magic potion. "After one drink they imagined themselves fiery green dragons and sleek running horses," this dad said.

Unused juice and soda pop, which will go flat if left in the can, can be added to gelatin.

The stray box of unsweetened cereal rejected from the variety pack often hangs around the pantry begging to be eaten. It can be used as a coating on chicken, or baked in the Nuts and Bolts recipe given on page 104.

Bits of leftover cereal (or wrinkly, unappealing grapes) can be added to cookie batter.

Slipping pennies between the inner and outer wrappers of a big cereal box can be used as a last resort to motivate children to eat the small amount left in the box.

Children can help prepare the following tasty recipe, which suggests a way to use leftover meats and chicken:

Half-Moon Yummies

This dough recipe is simple to make and easy to handle. Bring 2 3-ounce packages of cream cheese and ½ pound of butter or margarine to room temperature. Mash together with a fork then add 2 cups flour. Knead well. Refrigerate overnight. (The dough may be kept in the refrigerator for up to a week.)

To prepare the meat filling, let the children hand-grind leftover roast beef and sauté with onions in butter, margarine, or oil. Season to taste.

The chicken filling is made by combining 1 cup of finely chopped cooked chicken or turkey with ½ cup of sharp cheese spread. Add ½ cup of mayonnaise and mix well.

When ready to fill the dough preheat the oven to 375°.

Roll the dough out on a floured board and cut circles with a cookie cutter or the rim of a drinking glass. Put a tablespoon of either of the fillings on each round of dough. Fold in half and press the edges tightly together, sealing with cold water. Bake the meat-filled dough on an ungreased cookie sheet for 15 minutes or until browned.

Remnants of leftover dough can be filled with jam, folded, and baked in the same manner.

Imaginative Serving

A twelve-year-old boy who invariably complained about leftovers approached the meal with new interest when told it was a smorgasbord. His mother set up the height-adjustable ironing board and covered it with a tablecloth, and the whole family could reach to serve themselves from the clever buffet.

Other ways of spicing up mealtimes are given below.

Mealtime Decorations Kids Can Make

Keeping children busy making table decorations takes their minds off before-meal snacking and scrapping.

They can create unique place mats with paper doilies or construction paper. They can select a theme, such as "pirates" or "pink," around which to design table decorations. Black paper place mats with white chalk skulls and crossbones can be made for the "pirate" meal. Red food coloring added to white milk can be part of the "pink" meal.

Attractive place mats for a "western" meal can be made by stitching jean-style pockets on blue denim fabric. Red bandanna handkerchiefs tucked into the pockets are used as napkins. This same idea can be carried out with construction paper.

Intriguing napkin holders can be made by pasting paper Thanksgiving turkeys, Valentine hearts, or birthday cakes on colored plastic spring clothespins.

One child took pride in his solution to the void in the middle of the bright red jello mold. He poked plastic flower toothpicks into the plastic basket from an empty container of solid Jet Dry water spot preventer. The miniature floral arangement was set upon a bed of parsley in the perennial trouble spot.

Children who write out menus offering limited choices of beverages such as white milk, chocolate milk, or lemonade add variety to a meal and gain experience in printing and spelling.

Beverages can also be varied by putting a candy cane in a glass of milk or floating marshmallow "ghosts" with clove faces in hot chocolate.

Packing Lunches

"Packing lunches is such a bore," said a mother whose children flatly refuse to buy their noontime meal at school.

This mother varied her children's lunches by including the following:

—minted toothpicks

—commercially packaged wax bottles or toys filled with juice

—a boiled egg with a Humpty Dumpty face drawn on the shell

—a carrot wrapped in aluminum foil and tied on the ends with curly ribbon

—a miniature juice extractor, a paper cup, and an orange for making fresh juice

—small cans of frozen juice and a straw for warm-weather slushies

She also had fun varying the style of writing the child's name on the paper sack. For example:

Alice   *Perriiiiii*

Andy the Great   *Suzieeeeee*

Adding Interest to Meals and Snacks

Add a novel touch to breakfast by cutting oranges as a grapefruit half is normally prepared, filling toy saltshakers with cinnamon and sugar, or serving chicken soup or ice cream—just for fun.

Muffin-pan lunches break the tedium of that meal. Put chunks of meat in one section of the pan, chips, cheese, and grapes in others, and continue until all sections are filled.

Toothpicks and muffin papers add flair to an ordinary meal. Serve pieces of cheese or watermelon on

116

toothpicks. Or make mini-shishkebabs alternating pieces of cheese, luncheon meat, fruit, and cubes of bread.

Children might be motivated to eat peas if allowed to spear them with a toothpick that bears a frizzy cellophane decoration. These fancy picks cost half a cent apiece and miraculously convert a plain plate of fruit or cheese into a work of art.

Apple and marshmallow creatures can be built using toothpick "bones."

"Porcupine" fruit made with toothpicks can accompany an entree of "porcupine" meatballs.

For children and adults who don't like gravy rivers winding through their food, serve applesauce or cottage cheese in muffin papers.

Always top a colorless mound of cottage cheese with a bright red maraschino cherry.

Preparing lunches in a calorie-conscious household complicates the mealtime scene. A piece of bologna on a plate without its sandwich blanket is much more appetizing with a jack-o'-lantern face. A piece of cucumber is a nonfattening cracker substitute.

One mother recommends keeping cleaned carrot and celery sticks in the refrigerator at all times. She puts them out in a relish dish with ice cubes, or pops them in a cup-style ice-cream cone for outdoor snackers. Peanut butter spread on celery sticks is also a nutritious snack.

A weight-conscious teen-ager discovered a warm-weather substitute for ice cream by freezing a peeled banana wrapped in aluminum foil.

Nourishing apples offer endless possibilities for creativity. An apple cutter which cores the fruit and causes it to spread open like a flower is a must in any household with children.

Serve round slices of apple with red-hot cinnamon candies as a substitute for applesauce. Before eating, the children can make faces, wreaths, or candy-studded bracelets.

Apple dipped in honey is another high-energy treat.

One family serves cupfuls of apples, nuts, and raisins with a traditional surprise such as a Lifesaver, chocolate chip, or coconut bonbon in the bottom of the cup.

Conclude a youngster's meal with a fanciful popsicle made by freezing juice-filled balloons.

PART SIX

NEEDING TIMES

Creativity in human relationships ... is a form or manner of relating to others which admits of one's own uniqueness and at the same time respects a uniqueness and dignity in others.

> —Harold H. Anderson, *Creativity and Its Cultivation*

People Dealings

Skill in developing satisfying human relationships begins with the development of these skills at home.

Expressing Feelings

Homes are beehives buzzing with emotions which need to be aired. "We didn't talk about feelings when I was growing up," says a sensitive woman. "If my parents were angry with me I was supposed to figure out why. Because I remember the lonely frustration of that game-playing, I try to be open and honest with my kids."

Parents who continuously work at bringing feelings out into the open tell of the following incidents where ruffled feathers were smoothed or anger abated:

A mother who got up one morning and found the refrigerator filled with sticky streams of melted cherry popsicles decided not to yell at her kids for leaving the freezer door open. Instead she told them she felt just like they did when they already had five hours' worth of homework and the teacher assigned more. Her children understood her feelings and helped her clean up the mess.

A father who had just spent two hours in a hot attic connecting his daughter's stereo to an antenna was burdened with the task of putting the ladder and tools away while his child relaxed and listened to music. Instead of calling the child lazy and ungrateful he told her he felt tired like a big brown horse pulling a heavy wagon. "I feel overworked and in need of help," he said. His daughter willingly put his tools away and fixed him a glass of iced tea.

Parents need to point out to children that though anger may be directed at them, the reason for it is not always their fault.

A tired mother whose pleasant dinner hour was interrupted by a telephone call from her employer became increasingly annoyed with her talkative children. She used this opportunity to explain the chain reaction of emotions to her kids: an employer yells at an employee, the employee vents anger on a child, the child kicks a dog, and the dog chases the cat.

Some families prefer to vent their feelings with pen and paper. The mother of a fourteen-year-old who changed one summer's day's plans seven times, wrote the demanding child the following note:

Dear Patty,

After a day like today I feel like someone has been whirling me around and around and I'm very dizzy. Just as I regain my footing I'm whirled again.

A child, embarrassed because his mother scolded him in front of a friend, wrote her a note identifying his feelings:

Mom,

You made me feel just like you did the time we had company for dinner and I told them you were serving leftovers.

Encouraging children to describe their feelings in terms of colors or senses helps them pinpoint their emotions. One child, touched by his mother's hug after learning he was not invited to a friend's birthday party, told his mother she made him feel "like a warm doughnut."

A girl angered because her brother spilled her lemon shampoo described her emotion as "red like an angry bull."

A child who was called from her room to set the dinner table, even though her brother was in the kitchen, told her mother it made her feel "like a sizzling firecracker." Her mother replied, "I understand your feelings. I could just as easily have asked your brother to set the table."

Children need to be encouraged to express feelings about internal struggles. One mom and dad sensed that their son was wrestling with his conscience. Their boy had bought a magazine and kept the extra change he was given in error. He told his folks, "I felt like I was a rope being pulled at each end. I knew I was wrong to keep the money, but I wanted to. The parents acknowl-

122

edged the child's struggle, then accompanied him when he returned the money.

Parents who are tuned in to feelings will try to use their imaginations rather than their emotions.

A father whose child left the dinner table in embarrassment over a spilled glass of milk slipped a note under the youngster's door which said, "We'll all be 🙁 if you don't come back to the table." This note helped the child save face.

One mother recalls an occasion when her sensitivity to her child's feelings worked like a magic charm. He was working in the yard and kept getting the rake caught in the narrow space he was attempting to clean out. The noise of the rake slammed down revealed that he had reached the limit of his tolerance. Sensing the frustration of the sweaty child, his mother offered to fix him a cold drink instead of launching a lecture about treating the yard tools properly. After this boost the boy returned to the yard and completed his task.

Another child was criticized for being negative when she complained about the dumb lady that spoke at a school assembly. "I have a right to my opinion," the girl replied. She did.

Family members need opportunities to express feelings without any justification. Feelings just *are*.

Helping children verbalize their emotions contributes towards their understanding of themselves, their family, and the outside world.

Avoiding Conflicts

A family which freely discusses feelings can avoid potential conflicts.

The parents of three teen-age girls realized that tempers were apt to ignite during periods of change from one activity to another.

The mother was disturbed when she returned from work and her girls immediately pounced on her with requests to go to the store for skirt material, birthday gifts, or school supplies. It upset the father to be greeted at the door with appeals that he lend the car or repair a bike. Both parents were happy to comply with their children's requests, but they needed a few minutes to kick off their shoes, glance at the headlines, and readjust to family life.

The five of them sat down together and listed various times of transition for the children as well as for the adults. Potential flare-up times were:

—returning from work
—returning from school
—returning from a trip
—returning from a friend's house
—returning from a day at the beach
—Monday mornings
—the first day of summer vacation
—the day after a birthday
—let down periods after preparing for an exam or participation in a contest
—when a best friend moves away

After this discussion each family member developed a greater awareness of the others' need to readjust. T.O.T. became a distress signal in the family when one member violated another's time of transition.

Other causes of disagreement are related to stages in children's development. When are they ready to take

124

buses alone? When are they ready to ride bikes? When should they take piano lessons? Often the readiness signal comes from the children themselves.

One mother and father were indecisive about hiring an evening baby-sitter for their twelve-year-old. When the child proudly announced, "You don't need to get a sitter for me. I'm old enough to stay alone," the parents respected their child's opinion.

Parents who had decided in their own minds that their daughter was not old enough to date took their clue from the girl herself. Her calm acceptance when they told her she could not go to the movies with Mark was a confirmation of their judgment.

But calm acceptance of parental judgment is not always the case, especially during the teen-age years.

The parents of a sulking fourteen-year-old who was not allowed to attend an all-day rock concert with a friend, went to bed distressed over the confrontation with their child. The next morning the mother wrote the following note to her daughter and slipped it under her bedroom door:

Dear Sue,

All of us feel uncomfortable after an experience like last night's. It's too bad our pleasant evening together deteriorated. I guess we all felt like we'd lost our best friend.

These are transition periods of great magnitude. We understand that growing up is not always easy for you, and it's not always easy to reach conclusions that will be agreeable to all of us.

Dad and I spent a lot of time discussing your

attendance at the concert, and I'm sorry you were so terribly angered by our final decision. Nevertheless, you have no right to treat us like you did.

Because your friend's parents allow her more freedom than we think is right for you, we must all be prepared to deal with situations where one family's standards are very different from the other's.

Just try to remember that we love you and whatever we do is in your best interest.

> Love,
> Mom

By expressing family feelings and pointing out the elements involved in this conflict, the mother hoped to at least soften future disagreements.

Family Respect

Asked to name the single quality which contributed most to their family relationships, a couple married eighteen years agreed it was respect. "We always considered politeness and *pleases* and caring and kisses vital to our life together as a family," they said.

This family described two situations where they made an effort to show respect for each other's ideas and capabilities.

When one child told his mother he thought she was overcooking the Thanksgiving turkey, she suppressed her first reaction, "I've been cooking turkeys for fifteen years, and no twelve-year-old is going to tell me how to do it." Instead of shattering the child's self-respect she replied, "It has been in the oven a long time. Maybe I'd better check it."

When this couple's nine-year-old kept getting underfoot while they were hanging drapes, their exasperated first reaction was to say, "Why can't you ever stay out of the way?" Instead they said to the child, "You have a good sense of design. Take a paper and pencil and figure out a way we can rearrange the furniture in this room."

Another couple, parents of three, said, "We learned very early in the game of parenthood that a positive approach showing respect works better than a negative one which puts a child down. When their fourteen-year-old had a frustrating struggle deciding how to wear her hair, their statement, "Your hair l⌐' lovely," was more helpful to the child, at that moment, than "Look at this messy bathroom. There are ribbons and rubber bands all over the place. All you think about is your appearance."

When their middle child had a fight with her best friend, their support of her decision to call the girl and try to patch things up was more helpful than "Why can't you get along with anybody?"

Parents who tell their children, "You never do a good job of anything," "You're always in the way," or "How come you don't have more friends?" are destroying their children's self-respect.

One mother says, "Every time I was about to utter a statement that was critical of children, I tried to remember the motto 'Children need models, not critics.'"

A Changing World

Being parents requires constant readjustment to children's needs. "Just as we learned to deal with creeping babies they started to walk, and just as we adjusted to their being on their feet they walked out the door to school," said the parents of four young adults.

Being parents requires an alertness to what is happening in the space-age world. Today's children are growing up at a time when significant changes in values, institutions, and life-styles are occurring at a rapid rate. They need parents who can stand firm on major issues such as honesty and dependability but can be flexible about minor ones such as habits of work and styles of dress.

A schoolteacher father who nagged his daughter about doing homework on the floor with rock music blaring realized when the girl brought home a straight A report card that sitting upright in total silence was not a prerequisite for excellence in scholarship.

Parents who objected to their son's wearing blue denim overalls when he went to pay a cheer-up visit to a sick old lady realized when the boy asked, "Do you think Mrs. King will care what I wear?" that his compassion was more important than his attire.

Children need parents who are willing to reexamine their standards in the light of the changing world. They need parents who will love them, listen to them, and respect them, and who will pursue with them an imaginative search for ways to develop satisfying human relationships.